O'Donnell's Boneyard

A Novel by

Seamus Thompson

ISBN: 1-40332-098-5 (e-book)
ISBN: 1-40332-099-3 (Paperback)

This book is printed on acid free paper.

1stBooks - rev. 07/02/02

1

A cold autumn sun, orange tinted, slipped toward its bed in the sea while dusk clung by its fingertips to the cliff tops of Northern Ireland. The lighthouse at the western end of Rathlin Island tested its beam against the fading day and the mournful calls of curlews rambled aimlessly down the wind.

Thudding against the darkening sky, echoing and bouncing along the towering cliffs of black basalt with the energy of a late summer storm, thumped the irresistible beat of the bodhran. Maria Burke hurried to its rhythm, dodging little fingers of the sea that scurried onto the sandy path running along the base of the cliffs. The bodhran beat a wild rhythm that jigged across the foam-flecked sea:

> Thud-thud-da-da-thud-
> Da-da-thud-
> Da-da-thud-
> Thud-thud-da-da-thud-

"If he'd do a little less thumping and a bit more work," Maria thought aloud, out of breath, "he wouldn't be in constant trouble." Her long-legged, bare-foot strides carried her across rivulets and around smooth black rocks that humped out of the sand. Only when she saw him in the distance, sitting on a rocky ledge looking out to sea, did she slow her pace.

He saw her coming and the beat grew faster—

Thud-thud-da-da-thud-
Da-da-thud-
Da-da-thud-

"There you are," he shouted, waving, never missing a beat, "and did anyone ever tell you that you look like Princess Diana, what with your blond hair streaming and your long legs…"

"For the love of God, Kevin, stop beating that infernal drum for a sec…"

"It's not a drum; it's a bodhran, and it helps me think and relax."

"Well, it does nothing for my nerves."

He tossed the doubled-headed beater high into the air and caught it with the grace of a majorette. "Okay. Would that be food you've tucked away in that wee basket?"

"Aye, but you're not getting a blessed bit till you tell me exactly what you've accomplished here, and when McKensie can expect a report."

"McKensie who?"

"Stop it, Kevin! This is serious."

"All right. What's in the basket?"

"Shepherd's pie, scones and tea."

"Ah, good. I'll get the stove for a warm-up."

He went inside the cave entrance and returned with a small portable stove. Next he brought out two folding camp stools. Supper was soon warmed and served as they huddled around the stove while scores of gulls fluttered about their feet, squawking for a handout.

"You've spoiled them," Maria said, "and they won't give us a minute's peace."

2

"Aye, you're right," sharing his meal with the raucous, quarreling birds.

When the food was gone the gulls flew away and a dusky twilight settled over the water. The Rathlin Island light flicked its steady warning.

"Is your report nearly finished, Kevin? McKensie is really angry. You asked him to cover your classes for a few days but you haven't been back in weeks." Maria spoke softly, between sips of tea, looking at Kevin's tousled dark hair and crinkly smiling face. "Where do you wash up here?"

"In the ocean. And the report is finished except for a few details." He looked out to sea. "I just don't know what to make of some of my data."

"What's to make? The National Trust is paying half your salary to classify bones, so classify and be done with it."

A long silence.

"It isn't that easy. I think there's something more important than classifying bones in that cave." He hesitated. "I don't think I want to talk about it just yet."

Maria arched her eyebrows, tilting her head in that shy manner. "What is it? The cave is a typical neolithic burial cairn. They're all around us. You just happened to find one with bones."

"I know."

"Well?"

"It's not the cairn, it's the skulls. Would you like to see?"

"Not on your life. That place gives me the willies."

3

"The willies? Now isn't that an interesting scientific term for a psychologist to use?"

"The willies, the creeps, the pip—have it any way you want. What shall I tell McKensie?"

"Did he send you?"

"Of course not, but he knew I was coming."

"Tell him I'll be back on Monday."

"Thank God. Now what's so important about those skulls?"

"You'll be one of the first to know," he said.

"Know what?"

"I'll think about it."

"Well, McKensie must have a report. The National Trust is on his back. What will you tell them?"

"Oh, they can have their report. That's no problem."

"Then what is the problem, Kevin,"—beginning to lose patience—"you speak in riddles sometimes and I can hardly understand you?"

"A conclusion, my love, an inescapable, astounding, scientific conclusion that I may include in the report, or leave out, depending on how they speak to me."

"Who?"

"The skulls."

"Ah, that's it, Kevin, you've finally gone 'round the bend, beating that damn drum and playing in a cave with 5000-year-old dead people. Where do you wash these dishes?"

"Rub them in the sand then rinse in the ocean."

"When they finished the dishes, Kevin said, "It's getting late and you have early classes. I'll get my torch and walk you back to your car."

4

Maria slipped her shoes on and they returned along the narrow strip of beach in the fading daylight, hand in hand, she an inch taller, he holding her hand tightly.

"Thank you, Maria, for a lovely supper."

She squeezed his hand. "You'll be in on Monday, then, with a nice change of clothes and looking like a college professor?"

"Looking every bit the Protestant educator."

"Ah, I shouldn't have said that, should I? But you know how they are—they don't expect much from their token Catholics."

"Do you?"

She stopped and put her arms around him. "I expect the best. You're the smartest man I know. And the sexiest."

"Then screw the lot of them." He kissed her.

As she climbed into the car, she paused and kissed him. "Goodnight, my love," she whispered. "Be careful. I worry about you out here by yourself."

Kevin watched as she sped away into the dusk, then he turned and walked back to the cave.

He brushed his teeth in a mug of fresh water, undressed, and scampered into the sea. He splashed and danced and shouted in surprise as the cold wet took his breath away. Around him the sea foamed and flecked and lightning flashed in the eastern sky above Fairhead. After a few minutes, he stumbled out, toweled himself dry, and put on his old jacket and jeans. Then he sat down on a rock and tapped out a rhythm on the bodhran, a quieter rhythm, and muffled, the beat of a thoughtful drummer. The time had come to get serious. After a few minutes he tucked the bodhran under his arm and went into the cave.

The cave was actually a passage grave chosen by people of the New Stone Age, no doubt because the ground rose steeply to a high and dry rocky chamber that was beyond the reach of even the fullest tides. Cold fresh air from the outside was carried in through numerous natural flues that sometimes whistled softly when the wind blew from certain directions.

Two kerosene lanterns lit the inside, their feather-light smoke rising to the flues. One lantern sat on a wooden crate covered with pages of penciled data. Vernier calipers and a couple of steel rulers served as paper weights.

On the floor beside the crate was a sleeping bag, a smaller crate with a few scraps of soap, a faded towel and a heavy duty torch.

The other lantern illuminated hundreds of human skulls arrayed on natural stone shelves recessed into the walls of the chamber. A stack of bones was piled in one corner.

Kevin had selected a small group of skulls for special attention, and these were arranged on crates and wooden planks around his make-shift desk.

Kevin entered the chamber and sat down heavily on his camp stool facing the row of skulls.

"Good evening, ladies, gentlemen, and wee babes," he said aloud. He studied the skulls thoughtfully. "Thank you for sharing your home with me. Tomorrow I'll leave you in peace and I hope no one will bother you again."

He gathered his papers into a neat stack and set them on one side of his "desk". "You've given me enough data for a dozen reports—and some I'm not sure I know what to do with."

6

He leaned over and picked up a small skull. "I think I know what you're telling me, but I'm only a stones-and-bones man. Look at what I work with." He held up the calipers and a ruler to the gallery of skulls. "Who will believe me? It's a high tech world out there, full of geneticists, microbiologists, neurobiologists, and other highbrow types, and you should see the pricey equipment they work with." He held up the calipers again. "I can hardly afford these. So who'll believe me?"

Kevin returned the specimen to its place. "Let's sleep on it, huh?" He unzipped his sleeping bag and pulled off his sneakers and trousers. "I could be the laughing stock of the University of Northern Ireland. That wouldn't bother me but it might embarrass Maria…"

He snuffed out the kerosene lamps.

"…or you could make me famous and all sort of characters might come poking around…" crawling into the sleeping bag in the pitch dark…

"…or you might get me killed. Nobody out there really wants to know about this stuff. So think about it."

The wind whistled mournfully down the flues. Kevin O'Donnell curled up on his side on the hard ground, pulled the sleeping bag high around his head and went sound asleep.

2

Seated behind his large uncluttered desk, Brian McKensie, B.Sc., Ph.D., looked more the barrister or estate agent than the head of an academic division of a university.

"Please have a seat, Maria," he said, "you look fresh and beautiful this morning. Blue is your color."

"Good morning, Brian. Thank you. If I could have a moment of your time…"

"All the time you wish."

"It's about Professor O'Donnell…"

"He's returning to work, I hope?"

"He'll be in his office on Monday. Actually, Kevin's been working hard under really primitive conditions…"

"Really? I can only suppose that he enjoys what he's doing or he would have returned long before this."

Maria shook her head in exasperation. "How could anyone possibly enjoy working under those conditions?"

"Well, you can believe what you like, but I tend to think that Kevin O'Donnell is a slacker. This division is noted for its productivity. We work hard, we work as a team, and O'Donnell doesn't seem to be a team player."

"Or do you exclude him by sending him on assignments that take him off campus for such long periods?"

McKensie pouted. "Aren't you being just a wee bit unfair? He volunteered…"

"When no one else offered to do it, of course he volunteered. That's just like Kevin. Och, forget it, Bryan. How are Elizabeth and the children?"

"McKensie welcomed the shift in conversation. "They're fine. Malcolm and…"

A loud knock on the door and the secretary burst into the room, visible excited.

"His Grace is on the phone," she whispered in awe.

McKensie didn't quite comprehend.

"Aye, His Grace," the secretary insisted with emphatic nods of her head.

McKensie turned pale. He picked up the telephone. "Good morning, Your Grace, Brian McKensie here," trying to sound professional yet properly subservient.

Listening.

"No, Your Grace, I'm afraid we were not. The invitation went to Queens in Belfast.

McKensie's voice rasped with morning hoarseness but he was reluctant to clear his throat. The secretary tip-toed out of the room and closed the door softly. Maria rose and walked to the window, wondering whether to stay or leave.

"I'm not sure, Your Grace, possibly three or four institutions in the U.K. were invited," McKensie said, a little more in control. "I don't have the exact number".

Listening. A short nervous laugh.

"Well, we're the youngest university in the U.K., Your Grace, so we have a lot to learn."

A weak smile faded quickly from McKensie's face. He sat with the phone in his hand looking at his desk for a short time. Then gently, as if the caller might hear, he hung up the receiver.

9

"That was the chancellor," he said to no one in particular.

Maria didn't answer.

"He wanted to know why we weren't invited to participate in the Egyptian antiquities conference." He paused. "Well, one university from Northern Ireland was to be selected and everyone knew damn well it wouldn't be us."

"Don't sell us short, Brian," Maria said, "we may be young but we have talent and verve and…"

"People like O'Donnell."

"What do you mean by that?"

"Well, it's obvious, isn't it? They can't expect to use this university as an instrument of social redress and aspire to academic excellence, too."

Maria turned on him.

"Diversity is the mother of excellence," she said. "Look around the world." She walked to the door. "And if you're referring to the few Catholic faculty, Kevin O'Donnell is an exceptionally bright professor. I know; I had classes with him at Queens and he routed the competition. You'd do well to rid your mind of such stereotypes; they're unworthy of you. Good morning, Bryan."

When she had gone, McKensie tapped the desk top gently with the side of his fist. Damn! Just about the last person in the world he wished to offend was Maria Burke. She had class, that one, elegance.

He walked out to the secretary's desk and said, "O'Donnell will be back on Monday. Tell him I said to cool his heels in his bloody office until I call him. And he's not to leave the premises. No excuses accepted."

3

Across the Atlantic at the University of Florida, Karen Rolf picked up a stack of journal reprints from her desk and headed for class. Twenty years ago, with a brand new Ph.D. in microbiology from Penn State, Karen was hired as an Instructor at the Shands Medical Center of the University of Florida. She was young, ambitious, eager to advance her career. Soon after, she married David Rolf, a Gainesville attorney and land developer. She learned quickly about surviving in a medical school. She wrote grant after grant and earned a national reputation as a competent researcher.

With the encouragement of her academic department, she won a post-doctoral fellowship to Johns Hopkins to study molecular biology. She returned from her postdoc with important connections and a supreme confidence in her own ability. After many years of research and writing, her reputation was assured internationally and she became a busy, sought-after professor who still managed to teach classes and challenge students with her refreshing insights.

Karen was also an excellent role model. With her stylish auburn hair cut fashionably short, her fine features and wide, curious green eyes, she was the center of attention wherever she went. Even in her usual mode of dress (spotless lab coat) she managed to look crisply elegant. At age 48 Karen had reached her prime, physically and professionally, and could offer no explanation for her colleagues' lack of enthusiasm for her latest published research.

When the article first appeared in *Science*, Karen prepared to be inundated with requests for reprints. She had presented a set of thought provoking data, a riddle of sorts, that was bound to generate controversy. Yet few requests for reprints had arrived, and these were mostly from graduate students. Karen waited expectantly. A few more requests, then none, none at all.

For the first time in her academic life, Karen Rolf experienced self-doubt. Where had her thinking gone wrong? How to explain the overwhelming indifference of her peers who usually greeted her work with such enthusiasm? Karen brought the problem to her class of doctoral students.

She passed out copies of the article and assigned it for discussion at the next class meeting. When the class reconvened in a few days, Karen opened with general remarks and then plunged right into the topic.

"Let's talk about mitochondrial D.N.A.," she announced, "which is the subject of the paper you read. Why do we study mt D.N.A.?"

A general silence for a few seconds and then a reply from an Asian student in the second row.

"Mitochondrial D.N.A.—" she had trouble with the 'r'—"is inherited only from the mother."

"Like all D.N.A., it's found in the nucleus of the cell, of course?"

"No, doctor, not in the nucleus."

"Then where?"

Before the Asian had a chance to reply, another student spoke up. "In the mitochondrion of the cell."

"Since when?" Karen asked. "I thought all genetic material was found in the genes within the cell's nucleus?"

"Not since the 1960's."

Karen was pleased. "You're both on target. For the benefit of the lazy, the mitochondrion is the engine that produces nearly all of the cell's energy, and, strangely enough, it also contains D.N.A. material. Even more strangely, this D.N.A. is donated only by the mother. Why is it particularly useful in the study of genetics?"

The Asian was quicker this time. "Useful for tracing ancestry since it is not contaminated by paternal D.N.A."

"Contaminated?" a male student said. "Try hatching your eggs, darling, without paternal D.N.A."

"I remember the so-called Eve project at U.C.L.A. that got such media attention years ago," another student offered.

"Yes," Karen said, "that was an interesting case." To the class she explained, "In the fossilized remains of an ancient African human female the U.C.L.A. group claimed to have found genetic material that we still carry in our own D.N.A. after more than 200 thousand years. In other words, they thought that Eve might have been the mother of humankind."

"Yea, I remember that," said Nick, the laid-back, scraggly-bearded Doubting Thomas of the class. "I still wonder how they arrived at that conclusion. Sloppy research."

"Well, their work has been questioned," Karen said, "and you're right. It was sloppy research, but it was a tantalizing hypothesis, wasn't it?"

13

"I ran the same computer program," continued Nick, "and depending on the algorithm I used, I could put Eve in Asia, Africa, or even in Europe. That bit of research stretched even my imagination, and believe me, my imagination doesn't need stretching."

"But still an interesting idea, don't you think?" Karen asked.

"Not really, m'am. I study the same evidence as everyone else, and I find no single person responsible for the entire population of the world. That's a preposterous notion. I think an intermixing and intermingling of subspecies down through the millennia seems more probable. That business of Eve's descendents genetically wiping out everyone else—well, that's media hype. If we were all descended from the daughters of this Eve, then her daughters would have had the same maternal grandfather. Which would make Adam, Eve's father."

Karen threw up her hands. "Does anyone in here follow that logic?"

"Only the men," a female student quipped.

"It's called CNL—Convoluted Nick Logic," another said.

"Okay, back to today's assignment," Karen said. "This study…"

"Could I ask a methodological question?" a male student asked.

"Well, okay," Karen answered, "but please don't sidetrack us."

"Your study required a lot of body tissue in order to isolate sufficient mtD.N.A. My question—where did you get such large quantities of tissue."

"I wish all of you would read the assignments more carefully. I simply followed the U.C.L.A. procedure and convinced a lot of pregnant women to donate their placentas to science."

"Only a woman would have thought of that," a female student said admiringly. "There must have been a woman on that team."

"Well, I don't know about that," said Karen, "now, on to the study at hand. As you have read, originally I was engaged in some routine work on the genetic bases of certain aspects of the immune system when I isolated two distinct populations, genetically speaking, where there should only have been one. I found genetic material in 15 percent of my population that should not have been there at all. What this material does, or why it should be found in one population and not the other, these were the questions I posed in the study. Apparently the questions weren't interesting enough since few of my colleagues responded to them. Nevertheless, the questions stand."

"Were all of the women who donated placentas of the same ethnic background?" a student asked.

"No," Karen answered, "but it's long been established that all the human races are genetically similar, so we can rule out racial differences."

"Exactly what were the differences you noted?" another student asked.

"No," Karen answered, "but it's long been established that all the human races are genetically similar, so we can rule out racial differences."

"Exactly what were the differences you noted?" another student asked.

"Didn't you read the article, Donna? I found in 15 percent of the cases significant abnormalities in the molecular structure of blood protein."

"Well, what does it mean?"

The class hooted and howled. "Hey, Donna, where have you been? That's what we're trying to find out," they called out in unison.

"Okay, okay, settle down," Karen said. "Any ideas, Donna?"

"Did you make a mistake in your analysis? Maybe your equipment…"

"Not one hundred and fifty mistakes. One or two, maybe. No, I checked and rechecked my work and so did my graduate assistant. The results were the same. So I decided to toss the riddle to my colleagues, and that's why I wrote the article."

Again Donna asked the question that consumed the class: "But what does it mean?"

Silence.

"I'm glad we discarded the Eve hypothesis," Nick drawled, "or we'd never know what it means."

"And since you're not so burdened with Eve—?" Karen asked.

"If your study can be corroborated, then there's a possibility that once again some of us are mutating."

"Mutating?!"

"Why are you so shocked? It's been going on for millions of years right under our noses and you just happened to have the luck and skills to detect it. Do you want an hypothesis? There is a new subspecies of human evolving in our midst…"

Karen Rolf didn't hear the rest. Her green eyes stared in amazement at Nick, the class maverick, and somewhere deep within her fertile brain a burst of neurons exploded into an unthinkable possibility.

4

They were stocky and tough-looking, three of them, all in their 20's, and Kevin knew he didn't stand much of a chance if they forced a fight. Perhaps he could still talk his way out of it.

"Och, come on," he said, "it's Sunday morning. Who the hell needs this on his day off."

"We've told you before," one of them said, "to stay out of Glenards."

"Be sensible, man, my girl lives here. Now be decent lads and…"

Another shoved him. "Get back in your car and head out or you're in trouble, Sunday or not."

Kevin stood his ground. "I'm not looking for trouble, and for God's sake be quiet or you'll have the neighbors out. There's three of you and only one of me. What'll that prove?"

"Get back in your car."

Kevin finally realized he wasn't going to get off that easily. Even if he turned away, they'd probably jump him from the rear. Better to meet them head on.

"Well, let's bloody well get on with it then," he said, reverting to his old West Belfast street accent.

They were at him in a flash, punching, cursing, biting. He managed to drive a fist deep into someone's eye before they wrestled him to the ground.

The loud grunting and cursing brought out the neighbors who added to the din with their own shouting and screaming.

"Here, there, stop that!"

"Call the police!"

"Where are the bloody police—they're never around when you need them!"

Finally one authoritative voice cut through the melee. "That's enough. Get off him now, the three of you. MacAndrews, I'm not telling you again. Get off and let him up."

Kevin lay flat on his back looking up into the sunny October sky, cloudless and nippy, looking up into the frowning face of Phil Burke in his undershirt and black Royal Ulster Constabulary cap.

"Thanks, Phil," Kevin said.

"You're not a damn bit welcome, O'Donnell," Phil said. "I don't know what my sister sees in you anyway, but even you should be allowed to walk the streets in peace." Then he turned to the three youths "If you bother him again, I won't arrest you. I'll take you over to the fields and let you have a got at me. Do you understand, MacAndrews, since you seem to be the ringleader of this bunch?"

"Aye, sir."

"Stay here," Phil said to Kevin, "and I'll send Maria out."

"I'd like to come in and wash up a bit."

"They're having breakfast."

"Well, never mind. Just get Maria, then."

"Suit yourself." Phil strode away and the neighbors went back behind their window curtains.

Kevin was still brushing off his trousers when Maria rushed up.

"Oh, dear God, what happened?"

Kevin grinned, still a little shaky. "A thrill a minute courting you."

"Let's go inside and have a wash."

"No, thanks, I'll use the facilities at Ballintoy Harbour."

Maria was embarrassed. "Kevin, I'm sorry. We're just a wee town with a few bigots, but most of us are decent people." She dusted off the seat of his pants and whispered confidentially, "Och, haven't you the lovely wee bum."

Kevin smiled in spite of himself. "I'll let you see mine if you'll let me see yours."

"Cheeky bugger! Sure you won't have a wash up?"

"No. Let's go while the weather's nice."

"Okay. By the way," she asked, "did you go to Mass this morning?"

"No, I didn't."

"Serves you right, then. I thought all Catholics went to Mass on Sunday."

"Only the good ones."

"I've been under the impression that you were good at everything you did."

Kevin grinned. "Okay, you win. Mass every Sunday from now on."

"Good. If you're not going to be a good Catholic then you might just as well save the both of us a lot of trouble and join the Church of Ireland with me."

"Not likely."

Highway A2 hugs the cliffs of the north Antrim coast. The view is spectacular. On a clear day the dim outline of Scotland shimmers far across the water.

"Did you send your report to the Trust?" Maria asked.

"Aye, and a copy to McKensie."

"Did you let it all hang, as the saying goes?"

"Every bit. I laid it all out, for better or worse."

"Will it be controversial, your report?"

Kevin suddenly swung the car into the road leading to the ruins of Dunluce Castle. He pulled into the car park and climbed out. "Let's sit down here for a minute and enjoy the peace and quiet."

He led Maria to a stone wall overlooking the sea and the elegant ruins of Dunluce Castle, the once-great battlements of the Scottish clan of The MacDonalds. They sat quietly enjoying the beauty of the morning.

After a few moments, Maria broke the spell. "Kevin, my love, I'm truly sorry about this morning. I wouldn't have that happen to you for anything in the world."

But Kevin wasn't listening. Sorley Boye (Charlie the Fair) MacDonald, the most colorful of the clan, once salvaged cannon from the underwater wreck of the Spanish galleass, *Gerona*. Mounting the gun on the battlements, he beat off the attacks of the Earl of Antrim. Remarkable, considering the guns had first to be retrieved from underwater and then hauled up a sheer 200 foot cliff.

"Kevin! Are you listening?"

"Aye, I heard you. Sure, it wasn't your fault, Maria. But I'm glad Phil came along when he did."

"I know you won't believe this, but Phil really likes you. It's my mam and dad who cause most of the trouble."

"I like Phil, too, and I like your mam and dad. What do they want from me?"

"It's your brother, the one in Sinn Fein who's always getting his picture in the paper. They see no difference between Sinn Fein and the I.R.A."

21

"Sinn Fein is a political party."

"Aye, that's what the I.R.A. say. Who believes them?"

"I believe them, but what has that to do with me? I don't give a damn about either one of them."

"I know, it's just nonsense, but it's all the mam and dad talk about. Anyway, let's change the subject. The day's too lovely from arguing about the I.R.A."

He put his arm around her shoulders and she rested her head against him. "I love you," he whispered.

She raised her lips and kissed him, a cool tingling kiss that tasted of morning and the sea, a long, long kiss that drove everything out of his mind except his love for her.

"Maria, Maria," he whispered into her mouth.

"I love you."

"Marry me."

She pulled away. "Och, you said you wouldn't bring that up again for a while."

"Sorry, come live with me, then."

"You know I would, but it would kill mam and dad. They're so old fashioned."

"It's hopeless. Let's just jump off the cliff."

"Well, you're improving. The last time we sat here you were for throwing mam and dad off."

They sat quietly again, lost in their own thoughts. Suddenly Kevin said, "Do you feel this bone at the side of your head—this one?" He ran his finger through her hair. "That's the frontal bone of your skull." He pressed in and downward. "It extends down and meets the sphenoid bone here. The same on the other side."

He paused for a few seconds, feeling the texture of Maria's silky blond hair. Then he continued. "In about seven percent of the skulls in that cairn, regardless of age or sex, the frontal bone extended downward significantly longer than it should have, and this extension shortened the sphenoid."

"Meaning what?"

"Well, this is only a wild guess, but for each cell in the cortex—all 10 billion of them—there are seven or eight glial cells underneath carrying nutrients to it. I think the elongation of the frontal bones in some of the specimens made room for more glial cells. This means that people with elongated frontal bones were able to use the cortex more efficiently because of the extra nutrition carried by the glial cells."

"Or perhaps use new parts of their brains?"

"Maybe, all guess work, of course. Nevertheless, seven percent of my sample had elongated frontal bones and shortened sphenoids. That's a fact."

"Suppose for a moment your guess is correct—"

"And that the mutation has been transmitted genetically for the last 5000 or so years?"

"Yes. What does that mean?"

Kevin rubbed his hands together. "If you laugh, I'll drop you off this cliff…"

"Never, darling, never. Please go ahead."

"From *Homo habilis*, the first reputed member of our genus, to *homo sapiens sapiens*—us—every step up the evolutionary ladder, from subspecies, has been recorded in the shape and dimensions of the skull. Not big changes, mind you, just wee bumps here, missing ridges there, hardly noticeable, but all significant enough to mark a new subspecies of human." He paused to let his words sink in. "I think I've found a significant change." Then he whispered, "The bones don't lie."

"What are you implying, Kevin, that a new subspecies of human has been evolving among us for more than 5000 years, and we don't even know it?"

"It's a possibility."

"What's the rate of evolution, do you suppose?"

Kevin shrugged. "I wouldn't want to guess. I've only had a chance to examine a few modern skulls in the past week or so…"

"But you can guess."

"It's unscientific."

"Guess, damn it!"

"Between 15 and 20 percent."

Maria lapsed into stunned quiet. An occasional car passed on the road.

"I hope you know what you're talking about Kevin, because you're saying that 15 or 20 percent of the people living today belong to a higher order of humans. That means most of us are dinosaurs, doomed to extinction. Some of us use more of our brains, or use them more efficiently, than others? There are two subspecies of human beings living side by side, maybe even married to each other."

Kevin shrugged. "Two or more subspecies of humans have coexisted before, why not now?"

"And one species is advancing while the other is dying off? All humans are not equal? Some are more advanced than others? That premise alone, if it's true, could unbalance the world. Everyone will want to know who is which, the Prime Minister, the president of the U.S., your own brother, you and I. Can you tell which is which?"

"No. Only by actually handling and measuring the skull itself. I don't have the instrumentation to make such fine distinctions in the living skull."

"Thank God. Are you curious?"

"In a scientific sort of way."

"Which species do you think I am?"

"I don't care."

"What about McKensie?"

Kevin grinned. "Ah, interesting. By the way, I'm meeting with him and a representative from the National Trust."

"To discuss this?"

"I'm afraid so."

"Good luck," Maria said. Pause. "Seriously, Kevin—now be serious, damn it—what to you think is the significance of your work for people like us?"

He thought for a moment. "Hope. We're not the end of the evolutionary line, better humans are on the way."

"What do you mean, better humans?"

"Hell, I don't know, more intelligent, less animal, less belligerent, less greedy—I don't know. But I do know they're here, not yet in numbers to make a difference, but soon. Soon."

Then Kevin pointed to the seaward tower of Dunluce Castle. "Now there's a real puzzle. That's called Maeve Roe's tower."

"I know that. What does Maeve Roe have to do with it?"

"She was the banshee of the Irish McQuillans who were the original owners of the castle but lost it in battle to the MacDonalds. Maeve Roe refused to

25

leave.   She sweeps the tower on dark and stormy nights."

"And no doubt you've seen her…"

"And heard her."

Maria suddenly kissed him. "God save us all from Irish anthropologists who drop scientific bombshells one minute and talk about fairies the next."

5

Julian Zeiss, an active Zionist and head of the anthropology department at the University of Florida, had earned a world-wide reputation under the hot sun of Israeli digs. He was an an older man just a few years from retirement who usually wandered into his office about ten o'clock most mornings, poured a cup of coffee, smoked his pipe and read the newspaper for about thirty minutes. He generally disposed of departmental business before noon with a few letters, notes and memos. Weather permitting, he walked across campus to the cafeteria for lunch, returned in an hour to check his mail, and then went home for a nap. He was back again at 6:00 P.M. for evening graduate classes which lasted until nine-thirty or ten o'clock.

For many years his routine had remained unchanged and he grew abrupt and testy with anyone who interrupted it, even the celebrated professor from the medical school, Karen Rolf. Although he was still interested enough to be curious, he was seasoned enough to pass her by with a quick nod of unrecognition as she sat in the reception area of the departmental office.

"Dr. Rolf is waiting to see you, Dr. Zeiss," the secretary said as he passed them on the way to his office at the end of the hall.

"Good morning." Smiling. "All right. I've a few things to do and then I'll ring you."

He sipped his coffee unhurriedly and glanced through the paper, but he didn't light his pipe. He wondered what she wanted. One had to be careful of

27

these medical people. They paid each other exorbitant consulting fees but expected the rest of the university to supply them with free information and advice.

"Please send Dr. Rolf down," he called.

Karen held out her hand to him, looking starched and professional. "Thank you for seeing me, Dr. Zeiss. I'm Karen Rolf from the Department of Microbiology."

"A pleasure, professor. Please sit down. How may I help you?"

"Thank you. I'm afraid my work has taken me out of my own field and I need expert opinion on a couple of things before I can go on. I wondered if you'd be willing to share…"

The emerald green eyes of Karen Rolf fascinated Zeiss. She used them with all the guile of a woman who knew how to enchant men. Here is a beautiful woman, thought Zeiss. And dangerous. He said, "If I can help in any way…"

"Thank you so much. Really, I have just a few naïve questions, but I'll feel more secure proceeding on the basis of your expert opinion."

Zeiss was years past flattery, still…"Am I to be quoted anywhere?"

"Oh, goodness, no," Karen replied. "This is just to satisfy my own curiosity and sense of neatness."

"Good. Well, in that case, fire away."

"Well, I know what the literature says but I wonder what you say. Do you think that human evolution will continue, or are we at the end of the line?

The question caught Zeiss off guard. He was expecting a technical question but—well, not this. He mentally scanned the literature, glancing away from those demanding eyes while he tried to frame an intelligent answer.

"In my opinion, extinction is much more likely than evolution," he replied. "We don't allow nature to weed out the weak, we interbreed, and as a subspecies, we're overcrowded, underfed, and underfueled. No, dear lady, in my opinion further evolution of this subspecies of human is highly improbable."

"Looking back though the millennia, what has been the average life span of a species?"

Zeiss searched carefully for a textbook answer. "Perhaps just under three million years. In our own case, we'll be lucky to manage a third of that."

"Am I hearing you correctly, then? You're actually ruling out further evolution of *Homo sapiens sapiens*?

"I am."

"And what if evidence were presented to suggest that a new subspecies of human has mutated and is evolving?"

Thoughtful silence. "Then I'd be inclined to think that the data, or the procedure, or both, were flawed."

That was not what Karen Rolf wanted to hear. "Has there ever been a time when two subspecies of human actually coexisted?"

"Goodness, yes. In Mount Carmel in Israel we found evidence that Neanderthals, Cro-Magnons, modern man, and an even more primitive type lived together, perhaps cooperatively, in the same neighborhood. I'm sure they had no idea they were different subspecies of humans."

"Then what makes you so sure that it's not going on now?"

"Oh, it is to some extent, at least genetically."

At the word 'genetically', a bell went off in Karen's head. Now he was skirting her territory.

"What do you mean?" she asked.

"Well, let's take noses as an example. Most of the fossil evidence suggests that primitive species of human had small, rather flat noses. Suddenly here are Neanderthals with large, prominent noses. Neanderthals disappeared, but have big noses disappeared?" He pointed to his own distinctive profile. "Evidently not."

"So you believe that Neanderthals weren't killed off by the Cro-Magnons, they simply…"

"Intermingled and interbred with anyone around. Subspecies of humans blended and blundered into each other. We are—pardon the simplistic metaphor—a genetic stew of all that has gone before us."

Karen smiled and could have hugged the old man. "Nick should be here instead of me," she said.

"I'm sorry—Nick? Nick who?"

"Oh, just a graduate student with similar ideas. Everything you say makes sense, Dr. Zeiss, but why won't you then concede that the process of evolving and mutating may still be going on?"

"For the reasons I've given, dear lady. However…" looking over her shoulder to the sky beyond the window…"I try to practice science, not espouse a dogma. Scientists change; dogmatists already know the answers and never change." He looked into her green eyes. "I am only an anthropologist looking for answers. I could be, and undoubtedly am, wrong. And now you must excuse me, it's getting on time to take care of departmental business."

Karen rose. "How can I thank you? Not only have you given me the information I wanted, you've given me the courage to be wrong. Will you have lunch with me? I'd love to talk with you some more."

It had been a long time since Zeiss had an offer of lunch from a beautiful woman, but he turned it down.

"Thank you; you're very kind, perhaps another time. But I'd like to know what you're up to. Tell me, why are you so interested in human evolution?"

"I've written an article that summarizes some of the research I've been doing," Karen said. "The response has been less than enthusiastic. In an oblique way, the article touches on genetic evolution."

"I'd like to read it," Zeiss said.

"Okay." She thought for a moment. "I ordered so many reprints that they were cluttering up my office so I took them home. Suppose I drive home and get you a copy?"

"I wouldn't want to inconvenience—"

"No trouble at all. My pleasure. I'd be interested in your reaction. Shall I leave the article with your secretary?"

"Yes, please do." Zeiss rose and held out his hand. "Thanks for visiting. Please come again."

Karen felt better. She drove through the noontime Gainesville traffic, something she had steadfastly avoided for years. The morning had gone well. She had learned a little anthropology, but mostly old Zeiss had given her the courage to risk herself even if she might be wrong, a philosophy not easily practiced in a medical school, but certainly a realistic way to think of

31

science. She would rethink the whole process, stick her neck out and try again. As old Zeiss might say, that's science at its finest.

She pulled into her driveway but found it blocked by a long, sleek Lincoln town car. Silver. A small magnetic sign on the door read: "Deborah Parrish, Realtor".

"My God, is David selling the house again?" she thought.

She let herself in through the front door. David was nowhere in sight and the house seemed typically quiet and undisturbed. She listened carefully. Yes, she heard low mumbling sounds, or something, from upstairs.

She quietly mounted the stairs and stopped outside their closed bedroom door. The sounds were unmistakable now, David's low moaning and a woman's higher, audible gasping. No question now, no room for doubt.

Karen suddenly felt sick. Her hand trembled as she started to grasp the door knob, then hesitated. She didn't want to see.

Quietly, she tiptoed downstairs to her work room. She found the stack of articles and a sheet of scrap paper. She wrote: "David, please do that in a motel. Also, call maid service and have them move my things into the spare room overlooking the garden. Karen"

She taped the message to the front door where David was bound to see it, then closed the door quietly behind her.

Keys in hand, she began to walk back to her car. On second thought, she returned to the silver Lincoln. She chose the largest key on her key ring, and, beginning at the front of the Lincoln, scratched a long, wavering line deep into the silver finish.

"Bitch!" she muttered.

Karen climbed into her own car, backed out of the driveway and drove away, eyes flashing green fire.

6

Kevin's report circulated from reader to reader, tic-marked and initialed, but merely skimmed. Eventually it was routed to the archivists, one of whom actually read it. He sent it back to the previous reader with a note obliquely suggesting a closer scrutiny. Within days, the well-thumbed manuscript was hand carried to the office of Sir Arthur Devon, director of the National Trust.

Devon, who was an amateur botanist with a fair background in general science, realized that here was a hoax, a blunder, or a political hot potato that he wanted off his hands immediately.

First he had his own experts sift through Kevin's data for conceptual errors. Finding none, he called in the Trusts's team of anthropologists to weigh the merits of Kevin's observations and conclusions. Although they did not reach a consensus, there was enough support for Kevin's data to caution Devon that here was the beginning of a full-scale political headache. Next morning he caught a shuttle flight to Belfast and motored to the University of Northern Ireland. He handed the report personally to the chancellor of the university who quickly scanned it but failed to grasp its significance.

"What the blazes am I reading, Devin?" the chancellor complained, flipping pages. "It's Sunday, you know."

"A rather strange piece of work, Your grace. if it has-validity, the social and political implications are— important."

The chancellor set the report aside and looked Devon squarely in the eye. "Tell me what it says."

Suddenly Devon felt a little foolish. "The study suggests that—ah—two subspecies of humans may coexist today. One species may still be evolving, the other, perhaps our own, may be on the way to extinction."

"So what?"

"The newer species may be more advanced, better brain, heavier thinker, less homicidal—that sort of thing."

"Well, I still don't see…"

"Given the choice between a more intelligent species and an older, more primitive one, from which species do you think people would elect the members of Parliament, or say, the president of the United States, or even the chancellor of this university?"

Now the chancellor understood. "How might one go about telling which is which?" he asked suspiciously.

"O'Donnell—the author—doesn't address that issue except through a series of complicated measurements impossible to carry out on living beings. However, if the report is published, I'm sure others will find a way."

The deep significance of the report settled in on the chancellor. "So we may have a natural caste system built into the human race," he said, "and some of us, perhaps you and I, belong to the lower caste. Is that it?"

"Exactly."

"Well, that will never do."

The chancellor, a heavy-set man, ruddy-complexioned in his brownish tweed sports jacket, leaned back in his chair and laid a thick, pinkish hand on the report. "At least we can do something about this. You say your organization funded this, Devon?"

"Yes, Your Grace, and one of your faculty undertook it."

The chancellor pursued his lips. "Has anyone else seen it?"

"A few of my readers and the chairman of his division."

"Can you lose it, or table it, or something?"

"Hardly," Devon replied, "not for long. Eventually it will be published."

"If it is, Lord Devon, you and I will bear the consequences. The political fall-out could be...ah...considerable. Can we convince the author not to publish at this time?"

"I've talked with the division chairman. He says O'Donnell will be difficult to deal with," Devon replied. "I have an appointment with him to discuss it. Perhaps you would care to sit in?"

"I don't think so. I would hardly want to be put in the position of censoring my faculty's work. However, this report must not be published at this time."

"Easier said than done, Your Grace."

"Does the Official Secrets Act apply?"

"I'd hardly think so; only Whitehall could invoke that, and I think it may be premature to involve the government at this point."

"Can we do anything locally?" the chancellor insisted. "We're not so protocol-bound here in Northern Ireland, you know."

Devon hesitated. "Well, nothing ethical…"

"Damn ethics! We have a situation that could get out of hand."

"I'm told that O'Donnell has a brother who is active in Sinn Fein. If we could find a way to link the two of them, you might be able to invoke the Prevention of Terrorism Act. You could detain him for a few weeks and perhaps convince him not to publish, at least not for the present."

"I'll phone Creighton immediately and have O'Donnell picked up."

"Lord Creighton may not wish to involve his police in this matter. After all, no crime has been committed."

"Don't worry about that. The R.U.C. owe me a favor or two." He stood up and reached out his hand. "Goodbye, keep your chaps in line over there and I'll take care of things here till we learn how to handle this."

Lord Devon of the National trust grasped the offered hand, not at all sure that he was doing the smart thing.

****

Kevin and Maria huddled together on the seawall at Ballintoy harbour watching the breakers crash and foam against the rocks. The quay was deserted except for an elderly couple walking briskly toward their parked car. Although it was barely five o'clock, a darkening, chilly twilight had chased most of the day from the sky.

"Race you to the car," Kevin challenged.

For answer, Maria snuggled closer, clinging to Kevin's arm. "I'm not moving."

Silence. "We're the only damn fools left."

"I don't care."

The elderly couple reached their car, backed out of the parking slot, and began the slow laboring climb up the corkscrew road to the coastal highway.

"We have to go," Kevin insisted, "I have papers to grade, assignments to review, the usual…"

"So have I."

Then suddenly Maria jumped up and stretched, the salty foam stinging her face. "Let's run away," she suggested.

"To where?"

"Any place warm. Mexico. Bermuda."

"Aye, wouldn't that be nice? Meantime…"

Kevin stood and encircled Maria's slim waist. Their noses were cold to the touch but their lips were warm. Maria tasted salty as the sea.

A long, lingering kiss. Maria trembled.

"See?", Kevin mumbled. "You're freezing with cold."

"That wasn't from the cold."

The sound of a car grinding down the harbour road startled them.

"That looks like Phil," Maria said, surprised.

Kevin watched for a second or two. "It's Phil's car." They walked quickly toward the parking area.

Phil Burke had climbed out of the car by the time they reached him. He was muffled up in a heavy sweater and windbreaker. "I thought I might have missed you," he said, "anyone with sense would have cleared out by now."

"And did you drive down to Ballintoy harbour just to tell us we've no sense?" Maria asked. "What's up, Phil, and why are you looking so angry?"

He towered over the both of them, a big, troubled man, clearly agitated.

"Kevin O'Donnell, what have you been up to?" he demanded.

"Nothing much," Kevin replied, "we've been sitting here talking nonsense most of the day. What is it?"

Phil turned to Maria. "This one will get us all in trouble, so he will. I stopped by the police station this afternoon and overheard a conversation I shouldn't have." He stopped and glared at Kevin. "We've been given orders to pick you up tomorrow morning. You're to be held and charged under the Prevention of Terrorism Act. You know what that means—Long Kesh for weeks, maybe months, without benefit of lawyer or trial."

"What! Are you bloody serious, man?"

"Ah, Jesus, of course I'm serious! I'm risking my job just being here."

"But it's all damn nonsense. What could I possibly have done…"

"Someone wants you out of the way," Phil interrupted, "why, I don't know."

"It's that damn report," Maria said. "I knew there would be trouble…"

"They've nothing to hold me on," Kevin insisted.

"Don't be simple," Phil said. "While you were out here enjoying yourselves, they've been planting a box full of explosives and detonators in your digs. Your building is already under surveillance."

"What can I do?"

"Jesus, I don't know," Phil answered. "I'm on my way to Ballycastle for a jar. You never saw me. Is that clear, O'Donnell?"

Kevin nodded. "I understand. Thanks, Phil."

Phil climbed back into his car and sped away, leaving them speechless in the gathering dusk.

"Now what?" Kevin said, more to himself than to Maria.

"Oh, god, you'll have to go 'on the run' or it's Long Kesh for you, my darling," Maria said.

"Run where? I've no place…"

"For god's sake, Kevin, you were born and raised in Belfast. You must have learned something. Get across the border before they pick you up."

"But why? I haven't done anything. I'm completely innocent. Why should I run away?"

"Didn't Phil say they planted explosives in your digs? Must I remind you that this is Northern Ireland," Maria said, "and the authorities do as they damn well please with suspected I.R.A. members? Get across the border, darling. It'll just be for a few days till we get this thing straightened out and see what they want. Drive me home, then go quickly. Phil doesn't exaggerate. And for god's sake, Kevin, don't go back to your apartment. They'll be waiting to arrest you, and once they get their hands on you…"

Kevin sighed loudly and shook his head. "Doesn't it matter that I don't belong to the I.R.A., I don't support the I.R.A., I don't even like the I.R.A.?"

"It doesn't matter, Kevin. It's all a pretense to detain you for some reason or other.

"Jesus, it's like fascist Germany…"

"Or the Middle Ages. But we're losing time. Drive me home and then get across the border." She reached into her purse. "Here's all the money I have with me. I'll get more and take it to you when you let me know where you are."

Kevin drove to Glenards and kissed Maria a reluctant, perplexed goodbye. The early evening was dark, and lights gleamed in windows. "Tell me again why I have to do this," he whispered, "I still can't believe it."

"Because, my naïve darling, you don't want to spend months, maybe years, being brutalized in Long Kesh Prison." She kissed him tenderly and clung to him in the blackness of the little car. "It's only for a wee while, till you work it out. Phone your brother. He'll help. Goodbye, Kevin. Please don't give them any excuse to hurt you. And phone me as soon as you can"

Maria went into the house and Kevin pulled away from the curb. At the same time, two sets of headlights flashed on further down the street and drew close behind, almost blinding him in the glare.

Now it was too late to cross the border. The police were already tailing him and no doubt they had alerted all border crossings.

He drove slowly along the coast highway to Portrush road, turned left o Coleraine. The lights behind followed every turn. He pulled up and parked outside his lodgings. One car pulled in front of him; the other closed in behind. Kevin climbed out and walked casually back to the car behind. He tapped on the side window, but the driver, in plain clothes, stared straight ahead. Kevin shrugged, gave up, and walked back to his apartment. As he let himself in, his mind worked quickly. Phil was right; this was serious. At the crack of dawn he would be arrested and locked up. He had to get away.

7

Shortly after 2:00 A.M. Julian Zeiss closed Karen Rolf's paper and stood up and stretched. He walked through the darkened house to the back door and quietly let himself out to the patio. The neighborhood was middle-of-the-night quiet.

Zeiss knew he had to do something, but what? This Rolf woman had the scientific news story of the century, but he had to be sure. With some physical corroboration (which shouldn't be difficult to obtain) she could become famous. Nor were the implications of the study lost on Zeiss. This was the sort of stuff that could shake world politics.

He paced up and down the patio, thinking, juggling ideas. Somewhere in the dark, a dog barked. Where are you now, Sol Braverman, when I need you? Sol had an answer for everything. And people thought he, Zeiss, was eccentric! They should know Sol. Sol refused to do any kind of paperwork, refused to maintain an office ("An anthropologist belongs in the field!"), went off into the Israeli wilds for weeks at a time and took his students with him, and generally drove the administration of the University of Tel Aviv to distraction. But he put them on the anthropological map, so he was untouchable. Sol had the answers.

Suddenly Zeiss knew what he would do.

He hurried back to his study and glanced at the wall clock. Sol would still be at home unless he was somewhere out in the boondocks. Zeiss flipped through his personal telephone directory and hurriedly tapped in a set of numbers.

The overhead lights of the study blazed on and his wife stood in the doorway in her robe and slippers.

"My god, who are you calling at this time of night?" she asked.

"Sol."

"Sol?" She glanced at the clock. "What's so important it can't wait?"

The telephone played its confusion of tones. "Go to bed, Becky, I'll be up in a minute. This is shop talk."

"Do you want the light left on or can you hear better in the dark?"

Zeiss waved her out with his hand. "Sol? Sol! This is Julian." His wife tiptoed out of the room. "That's right—Julian. How are you? Listen, Sol, I have a paper I want you to read. A research paper. No, Sol, this is heavy stuff, it can't wait. No, Sol, I don't care where you're going I want you to read it now, this morning. Give me your fax number."

Zeiss waited impatiently. "All right, I have a pen." He scratched some numbers onto a piece of paper.

"Listen, Sol, go to the office and wait for me. I'm going to my department right now and fax this paper to you in thirty minutes. Thirty minutes, Sol. No, it can't wait. Can't you tell how agitated I am that it can't wait? Go, go, right now. I'm leaving, Sol. I'm leaving. Phone me when you've read it. All right, Sol." He hung up the phone.

Zeiss quickly dressed and drove to the university. The campus was quiet and deserted except for a few lights gleaming in dorm windows and a radio playing softly in the distance. He unlocked the door to his building and climbed the dark stairwell to the departmental office on the second floor. He flicked on the lights, glanced at the clock, then dug through the top drawer of the secretary's desk for a staple remover.

Within minutes he had separated Karen Rolf's paper into individual pages, dialed the number Sol had given him, got the okay from the fax machine, and began to feed in the report, page by page. He didn't hear the security guard who had entered quietly with gun drawn.

"Who are you, sir?" the guard demanded quietly.

Startled, Zeiss looked up. "For god's sake, put that gun away, young man." He fed another sheet into the fax machine. "I'm Julian Zeiss; I chair this department." He nodded toward his name on the wall plaque.

"Do you have identification?"

"Certainly, but I can't stop in the middle of this to give it to you right now. In a minute."

"What are you doing, sir?"

"I'm faxing a document."

"In the middle of the night?"

"In Tel Aviv it's the middle of the morning. Now please put the gun away. You make me very nervous."

The security guard holstered his weapon and sat down in a chair beside the fax machine. He picked up the title page. "This is Dr. Rolf's paper," he said.

"Yes, I'm sending a copy to a colleague at the University of Tel Aviv."

Zeiss received confirmation that the paper had been copies correctly at the other end.

"Your identification, sir?" the guard insisted.

Zeiss handed him his driver's license and faculty I.D. card. The guard copied the numbers and handed the cards back. "Thank you."

"Will you see that the office is locked up before you leave?" Zeiss asked.

"Yes, sir."

"Goodnight, young man."

"Goodnight, sir."

Zeiss couldn't sleep the rest of the night. He drank coffee and finally dozed off in his recliner. He was awakened by the screeching brakes of school busses and the noise of children boarding. Dogs barked and sunlight sprinkled the room with dancing shafts of daylight.

"Coffee!" he bellowed.

"Don't yell," his wife answered from the kitchen, "I'm deaf? Coffee's on the table."

For the first time in years Zeiss phoned his office that he would not be in. Since he didn't have an evening class to prepare for, he sat around the house reading and rereading Karen Rolf's paper. He concluded that he was absolutely right; this was one of those research projects that had significance beyond the world of academe. He waited all day for Sol to confirm his judgment, but the phone didn't ring.

In the afternoon he went for a stroll, putting his phone on the answering device. He warned his wife that under no circumstances was she to answer or touch the phone till he returned. He walked a few long blocks trying to visualize what Sol was thinking and doing. Sol would see the significance of the study immediately. But then what?

He returned a short time later and rushed into the study hoping to find a blinking light on his answering machine. But the little red light glowed steadily. In fact, the call didn't arrive until eight o'clock in the evening when he had given up all hope of hearing from Tel Aviv that day.

"Professor Zeiss?"

Zeiss guessed from the connection that this was not long distance. "This is he."

"And how are you this evening, sir?"

"Very well, very well, indeed." This was not Sol. Get on with it, goddamn it.

My name is Joseph Hecht. Tel Aviv has asked me to call you about the research paper you sent Professor Braverman."

"Ah, yes, I was hoping to talk with Sol."

"Yes, of course. Dr. Zeiss, they tell me that you're an old friend. You've spent a lot of time at the University of Tel Aviv…"

"Ah, yes, very good times with very good friends…"

"And that Professor Braverman has promised you an adjunct professorship when you retire?"

"Well, ah, yes, in a way, but nothing signed, of course."

"We're delighted at the arrangement and we hope you'll come and stay with us when you're read to retire."

"Thank you, Mr…"

"Hecht, Joseph Hecht. Now about the paper. The Israeli government would like you to discourage Dr. Rolf from any further development of her ideas. Our experts here tell us that she will need evidence from anthropology or related fields to confirm her study. We hope that you will discourage her from seeking it, and if she disregards your advice, we would like to know immediately. Do you have a pen handy?"

"Yes."

"Copy this number, keep it in a secure place, and call me immediately in all matters pertaining to Dr. Rolf's study. Do you understand, Professor Zeiss?"

"I'm not sure what you're talking about."

"I want you to phone me if Dr. Rolf does anything more with her study. Just keep an eye on things for us. We have other friends in Gainesville who will also be watching, but no one in a position to influence Dr. Rolf directly. If you can, we want you to convince her to stop work on the study."

"But why? This is an important piece of work."

"Professor, I'm sure you realize the implications of the research. It transcends personal and professional feelings. Are you a friend of Israel?"

"Yes, of course."

"Then it's time to act like a friend, and, as you know, we show our gratitude in many ways. We are asking you to monitor Dr. Rolf's activities for us and to confide in no one. Absolutely no one, Dr. Zeiss. As you say, this is a serious piece of work. That is why Professor Braverman came to us immediately."

"When can I talk to Sol?"

"When we are certain whose side you're on. Meanwhile, don't attempt to talk to him or anyone else about our conversation. Is that understood? I'm your only contact in the matter of Karen Rolf, and I'll expect to hear from you soon and on a regular basis. You have my phone number. Call me."

"I see," Zeiss mumbled, unsure of himself.

"Good. Now please go about your work in the usual way and don't draw attention to yourself or to Rolf's study. Questions?"

"How can I ask questions when I don't know what's going on?"

"Thank you for your cooperation, Dr. Zeiss. Goodnight."

Zeiss hung up the phone. His hands shook as he unlocked a desk drawer and carefully hid the paper with Hecht's number on it. His hands shook because, somehow, the mysterious voice of the Mossad had reached half way around the world and, of all people, spoke to him.

8

The storm raged eastward out of Donegal and overwhelmed the final wisps of daylight. Rain spat furiously against the windows of Kevin's apartment and great gusts of wind roamed the dark streets of Coleraine shaking and worrying everything in the way.

Kevin sat with his hand on the phone trying to decide if the line had been tapped. The weather settled the issue. If he didn't phone Maria soon, the lines would probably go dead. He took the chance and Maria answered.

"Kevin!" She was shocked. "Where are you?"

"I'm home."

"Oh, dear god, I thought you'd be on your way…"

"Too late, Maria. Two cars were waiting for me on your street and followed me home."

Maria sighed. "Och, Kevin, poor dear. Did you get back before the storm?"

"Aye, it broke just after I got here."

"Well, darlin', you tried. Is this line monitored?"

"I don't think so. If they're going to arrest me in the morning, why bother?. Are you alone?"

"Aye, mam and dad went to bed early." She paused. "Oh, god," she whispered. "Tomorrow do what they want and be done with it. Everything happens for the best, anyway."

A long pause.

"Kevin?"

"I need the respect, Maria, and publishing's the only way open to me. I've found something important. It should be published."

"Respect? Respect? Are you daft?"

"No, I'm just a token Catholic trying to work at a Protestant university. I have to be better than anyone else. Just as good won't do. You know that." He paused. "That's the way it is with tokens."

Silence. "I thought I knew you, Kevin O'Donnell. Is this respect worth your career, maybe your life?"

"Oh, aye, respect's the only thing worth a life. Ask any Catholic."

"Och, Kevin, my love, I'm trying to understand how you feel but that's not possible, is it?"

"Not unless you're a token somewhere."

"Aye, but for our sake couldn't you just study and teach, and bide your time? You're good; your day will come." Pause. "Where are the policemen who followed you home?"

"They're outside blocking my car and trying to keep warm, poor sods. It's raining buckets and the wind would blow you away, so it would."

"Kevin?"

"Aye, Maria?"

"I hear that strange sound in your voice. Do you love me?"

"You know I do."

"Then don't do anything foolish, please, for me?", Maria begged. "You're not cut out for life 'on the run'. You've no safe houses to go to or the usual network of friends. The weather's foul and it's going to stay that way for days. Kevin, are you listening?"

"Aye."

"You'll perish out there. The R.U.C. or the Brits will pick you up before morning. You can't go to your brother's and you can't go back to that cave. Besides, you've no money, no decent warm clothes, you can't take your car…"

"Och, Jesus, Maria, don't you think I know all that?"

"Then promise me you'll go to bed, and tomorrow you'll do what's necessary to make peace with them. Promise me, Kevin."

Kevin said, "Goodnight, Maria. I love you." He hung up the phone and disconnected it from the wall.

He turned out most of the lights in the apartment. In the semidark he loaded a backpack with food and a blanket. Then he bundled himself in the foul weather gear an anthropologist always keeps handy. He picked up his bodhran and tied it to his back pack, covered everything with heavy plastic, and slipped his arms through the straps. He adjusted the load. Heavy, but he could manage.

He took a last look around at the things that gave him comfort, the old faded photo of his mother and father, Maria's picture, his books, his records, the second-hand recliner where he read and dreamed of a family of his own. Ah, well, it wasn't the end of the world, was it?

He quietly opened the back door and the wind nearly tore it off its hinges. Rain pelted him in the face with huge stinging drops that chilled him to the bone. He closed the door behind him, hunched his shoulders and lowered his head, and staggered into the storm, almost wishing he had listened to Maria. But he had come this far, hadn't he? He'd never turn back.

9

A gale off the Antrim coast in the light of day is a splendid fury, but in the dark of night, a terrifying confusion of booms and crashes, howls and moanings, and the rattling of things never meant to rattle. Rain pounds jagged off-shore rocks and whips the air with stinging wet tendrils. Mountainous waves roll in from the frigid oceans of the arctic and smother the base of black cliffs in blankets of glowing foam. Howls and screams and ferocious gusts—Kevin O'Donnell wondered how any living thing could last through such a night.

He battled the wind and rain that savaged the deserted coastal road. His teeth chattered and his body shook from the bitter cold and wet. He kept to the center of the road, safer there, and he could make better time. Only once did he scurry clumsily into the shadows when a small auto, yellowish headlights barely seen, splashed and skidded past in the gloom. Chilled to the bone, dripping wet, aching in every muscle, he slogged along, step by step, sometimes helped by the howling wind at his back, continually blinded by the rain.

Hour after weary hour, making slow erratic progress, blown this way and that, stumbling…

At last he saw, no, rather, he sensed, Dunluce, the one peril was ending but another just beginning. Black against a blacker sky, the jagged outline of Dunluce Castle rose out of the night while far out on the western sea thunder growled in the dark of Donegal.

Kevin turned left into the grassy field that led to the edge of the rocky promontory. The ruins of Dunluce Castle, rain-drenched and sharply drawn against the sky, rose to his left. He wouldn't enter the ruin itself. The roofless old structure offered no protection and no safe hideaway. He would, instead, try to descend the narrow rocky path that angled down the face of the cliff to the sea below.

He remembered the first time he and his older brother, Barry, had ventured down that dangerous path during a Portrush holiday. Barry had told him wonderful stories about the cave entrance to old Dunluce Castle and how Sorley Boy MacDonald had kept a boat anchored there to escape by sea if his enemies breached his defenses.

Even in the light of day the path was steep, slippery, and cluttered with things to snag the feet as one clambered down the almost-vertical face of the two-hundred foot cliff. He remembered calling out to his brother when the height terrified him, and Barry came back and led him by the hand through the more dangerous places.

To descend that path in the dark, in a raging storm with wind gusting at 40 to 50 miles an hour, terrified Kevin. But there was no choice. Below was safety and refuge from the storm, the path was the only way down. Carefully he stepped over the edge and felt the first rocky step underfoot. He crouched as low as he could, groping for the next step while the wind tried to tear him from the face of the cliff and send him plummeting into the raging sea below. One step at a time, he told himself; don't try to hurry, you have all night. He felt the next step, and the next.

Slowly, cautiously, crouching low and feeling his way in the profound blackness, Kevin descended the slippery, narrow path. Around him the wind screamed and the rain lashed him mercilessly.

And then suddenly his outstretched foot felt…nothing. Frantically he groped. Nothing. Then angling himself sideways on the narrow step, he felt with his hand. Nothing. Suspended halfway down the face of the cliff, he didn't dare step down without feeling something solid underfoot. For all he knew, the torrents of rain could have washed the rest of the footpath into the sea.

Carefully, he leaned backward, feeling with his hand for the step above. Then he hunkered down and slowly eased himself into a sitting position. The backpack pushed him dangerously forward as he searched the pockets of his jacking for his small torch. He found the torch but its dim light, barely perceptible in the overwhelming darkness, revealed that the next step down was missing, probably washed away. A mud slide, nearly vertical, dropped downward for about four feet to the next stone step.

Kevin turned off the torch and sat quietly, eyes closed, tired and frustrated while the storm raged around him. He considered trying to climb back up the foot path, but then what? By daylight he would be in custody. But the choices below weren't so great, either. At best he might have a day or two while he tried to sort things out. At worst he could plunge to his death in the darkness, and he had to make up his mind quickly or the wind would settle the matter with sudden finality.

He couldn't slide down the mud with the backpack on, so that was the place to begin. Barely breathing, with small, calculated movements, he angled himself sideways and slipped his arms out of the backpack, unzipped it, and felt inside for the manila envelope containing his report. He found it, folded it, trying to keep it as dry as possible, then stuffed it into the inside pocket of his jacket. He released the backpack and let it fall away from him, bouncing and bumping into the darkness below. Nor could he hold the torch and slide down at the same time, he needed both hands to balance himself as he pressed backward against the cliff. He would have to pocket the torch and slide down in the dark.

Gripping the torch as steadily as he could, he took one last look at the place where he wanted to land, trying to visualize every important detail. One missed footing, one miscalculation—all the memories of the terrible vertigo of years ago returned and for a moment almost paralyzed him. Reluctantly he turned off the torch and slipped it into his pocket. He dug his heels into the mud and slowly, gently, pushed off.

Then two things occurred almost precisely at the same time. His feet struck the rocky step below exactly as he had planned, but the step gave way, loosened by the rain, and plunged downward. The second event saved his life. A savage gust of wind blew in from the sea and pinned him, arms outspread and grasping desperately for a handhold, to the face of the cliff. He gently slid downward, fastened to the cliff by the wind, till his feet touched solidly on a step below. And then the gust died away just as suddenly as it had arisen.

Kevin rested for a few seconds, not knowing what to expect next. His heart beat so heavily he could feel it pounding under his jacket. "Oh, god; oh, god," he said aloud. In his mind he saw himself falling, endlessly tumbling, into the awful maelstrom below.

Very slowly he bent his arm and felt in his pocket for the torch. The feeble light revealed that he had slid about six feet down an almost vertical mud embankment, and that his foot was resting now on a stone step. The light also showed another step below, and another after that, descending into profound blackness.

Kevin realized that he must keep moving; minute by minute the steps were being undermined by torrents of rain. He took a deep breath and then stepped down to the next foothold, and the next, hands clutching for anything that might help him balance himself, descending faster than was prudent. He wanted off that cliff and into the cavern below.

When the torchlight illuminated a narrow stone ledge sloping down to his left, he breathed a little easier. The ledge was about ten feet above the water, and, after turning a corner, ran directly into the water-filled cavern beneath Dunluce. Even as he watched, however, another peril arose. An occasional rogue wave broke over the ledge with hissing, crashing fury. If a wave caught him before he had time to find a suitable handhold, he would be swept away. Don't think of it, get across as quickly as you can, and into the cavern. He remembered the cave as a calm harbour in a while and stormy sea. The rocks blocking the entrance served as an efficient breakwater.

Kevin took a deep breath, waited for a lull in the wind and breaking waves, released his hold and stepped onto the foot-wide ledge. He took a few cautious steps, testing, then broke for the safety of the corner where the ledge made an almost-ninety-degree turn. Suddenly he tripped when his foot became snared and he sprawled onto the narrow ledge. He could have cried in frustration. A second or two elapsed while he recovered. Cautiously, he reached backward to untangle his foot and his hand closed around the strap that he had used to lash his bodhran to the backpack. He tugged harder. The backpack was gone but the bodhran and beater were still held by the strap. A miracle! He untangled his feet from the long strap, and, lying on his stomach on the ledge, pulled the bodhran toward him.

Then a monstrous wave, like a black wall topped with a fringe of glowing white froth, rolled in from the sea and thundered down directly on top of him.

Later when Kevin had time to think, he realized that if his foot had not become entangled in the strap, if he hadn't fallen flat at just the right instant, that wave would have plucked him off the ledge and carried him out to sea.

For the moment, however, he was trying desperately not to drown. Black-green water smothered him, swirling, sucking, roaring in his ears, first smashing him against the face of the cliff and then tugging and pulling, trying to pry him off the ledge. But he held his breath and braced his hand against the edge of the ledge, aware of the bodhran beneath him. Knowing that sooner or later the mountain of water would subside and rush back to the sea.

An eternity passed before the water retreated, hissing and gurgling, while he choked and coughed and tried to hold on to the ledge.

"Oh, god," he complained, "what next?"

He staggered to his feet, dripping wet but still grasping the bodhran, and stumbled toward the corner, talking out loud to himself.

"Now, damn, give me a break." He crabbed along the ledge in the pitch dark with a torch too wet to light, groping and feeling with his foot for the corner, one eye glancing fearfully toward the dark ocean, dreading the wall of water that might come at any moment...

The ledge turned left abruptly at an acute angle. Quickly Kevin rounded the corner and entered another world, no rain, no wind, just cavernous creaks and groans. He scurried deeper into the mammoth cave.

The ledge ended at a flight of stone steps leading upward, and, even in the pitch dark, Kevin knew exactly where he was. The steps ended abruptly somewhere up there in the gloom. The part of the castle to which they were originally attached had fallen into the sea centuries ago. But thirty or forty steps up, there was a wide ledge chiseled into the rock, evidently meant to be a resting place perhaps for women and children while the men made ready the boats below. He and Barry knew the place well. Once he had begged Barry to camp there. Naturally, Barry had refused because the interior of the cave, without railings or handholds of any kind, was a dangerous place.

Kevin reached the rocky landing and sprawled out, wet, face down, on the hard, uneven surface, completely exhausted. Later he would think about his situation.

Outside the wind howled and the sea pounded and raged against the rocks.

10

The R.U.C. station at Glenards, a small stone building wrapped in a tall chain link fence topped with barbed wire, dripped with early morning rain. Dim yellowish lights gleamed behind the few barred windows.

The chief constable sat behind an old oak table cluttered with paper and glared with open disgust at the two plainclothes men standing before him.

"Two of you," he said, "I posted two of you, not to mention two cars, and you let him get away." The chief shook his head. "Of all the donkey-eared, stupid..." He glared at them. "How did he do it?"

They looked at each other. "The storm," one of them said, "the wind and the rain, and the bleedin' cold, we never thought he'd make a run for it on a night like that."

"It was bad out there, chief," the other added.

"You were under the blankets, weren't you?" the chief said. "You were snoring away, farting, and munching your scones. And he gave the both of you the slip, and him a bloody professor with as much street sense as a bishop in a brothel."

"Sorry, chief," one of them said.

"Sorry my roaring red arse! I'll pay dearly for this and so will you. As of now, you're both suspended, without pay, for dereliction of duty. And I don't want to see either of you again till you walk through that door linking Professor Kevin O'Donnell between you. Do you understand me?"

The men were speechless. "Aw, Jesus, chief…" one of them began.

"Shut your flamin' yap!" The chief's face was beet red. "You let him go, now you get him back. And I don't care how you do it or in what condition you return him. Understand?"

"What about the stuff in his lodgings? Do you want us to get it out?"

"What stuff? I don't know what you're talking about. And if I were you I wouldn't tamper with evidence. Questions? No? Well, then, get the hell out of here and don't come back till you have O'Donnell, or until I read his obituary in the paper."

Both detectives, in their early fifties and veterans of the force, were married and supported teen-age children. They hadn't expected suspension without pay. They sat on a bench in the dark hallway trying to cope with the gravity of the situation.

"No pay. Jesus. What'll I tell the missus?"

"How the bloody hell would I know, haven't I the same problem? I'm going to turn over every bloody rock on the Antrim coast till I find that fly wee son-of-a-bitch."

"Where do we start, Seamus?"

"In Belfast. He'll make for the only family he has, that crafty bastard of a brother of his, what's his bloody name…?

"The Sinn Feiner? Barry O'Donnell."

It was a dirty day, windy, rainy and biting cold, so the trip to Belfast was thoroughly uncomfortable, especially so since the only car available to the detectives had a broken heater. Their teeth chattered when they finally swung off the M1 motorway onto the Donegal Road, and then up to the Falls Road.

"Turn onto the Whiterock Road, just before the Falls Park. Right there," Seamus said.

Barry O'Donnell, a tall, lanky man in his early forties with steely blue eyes and jet black hair and beard, opened the door and immediately took his visitors for the police. He stood in his stocking feet, one hand in plain view, the other grasping the gun on a ledge recessed into the wall just above the half-opened door.

"Police," they said.

"Och away!" he replied. "Who would have thought? And what will you be having, gentlemen?"

"We have a warrant for your brother's arrest."

And Barry O'Donnell, who had taught his face to reveal nothing, was caught off guard. The detectives saw the fleeting look of surprise and knew the trip was in vain. O'Donnell wasn't here.

The detective named Seamus, eyes darting about like a ferret's, asked, "Where might he be?"

"And what are you wanting Kevin for, sure isn't he at the university?" Barry asked.

"He's wanted for terrorist activities; explosives were found in hid lodgings."

And Barry O'Donnell had the first good laugh in weeks. He doubled over, trying to control himself, while the tears rolled down his cheeks. Finally he blew his nose loudly and got a grip on himself. "Sorry, lads," he said, "but you've no idea how funny that is." He started to laugh again. "Kevin wouldn't know a detonator if it came in his package of Smarties."

Seamus' eyes drummed the air nervously. "You won't think it's so funny when he's doing his time on H-Block."

Barry sobered up quickly and gave Seamus a long, cold look. "You've got the wrong man. I know my brother, and he knows nothing about explosives. You have my word on that."

"Your word? And who the hell are you that your word's worth anything?"

Barry opened the door wider and stepped outside, tall, dark, menacing in his full black beard. He said softly, "You're not in Coleraine now, you're on the Falls Road, and on the Falls, my word is not lightly questioned."

The other one pulled Seamus away. "Let's go; he's not here and we're wasting time."

Barry watched them drive away, wondering what Kevin had gotten himself into. He thought he had tucked his brother safely out of harm's way at the university. He went inside to make a few hurried phone calls.

The return trip to Coleraine was just as miserable. The detectives stopped for a cup of tea at a place just outside of Ballamena, and then continued the cold, uncomfortable ride back.

"The university," Seamus said, "that's the next place. Maybe we can find out something from his girlfriend."

"We'll want to tiptoe around her, what with Phil Burke."

Seamus glared at the driver. "Listen, Maguire, we've a job to do, Burke or no."

"Aye," Maguire replied, "but we'll still tiptoe. We've no official status, you know, what with the suspension and all." His false teeth chattered when he talked. "I'll take care of Miss Burke. You keep your eyes open."

They were stopped at the security hut at the entrance to the university but they showed their badges and were waved through. They found Maria in the library.

"We'd like a word, if you have a sec, please," Maguire said.

Maria put her journal aside and looked across the table at the two detectives. She recognized both of them.

"You're still working, are you?" she said. "I had lunch with Phil and he said you'd been suspended. I'm sorry to hear that."

"Aye, well never you mind your small wee head about that," Seamus chimed in, "we'll get by."

"Have you seen Professor O'Donnell recently?" Maguire asked.

"Not since yesterday."

"Do you know where he is?"

Before she had a chance to answer, Seamus interrupted. "Harbouring a criminal is a serious offence."

"Oh, I'm sure it is," Maria said. She turned to Maguire. "I believe you saw him after I did."

"I'm told he's been working at a cave near here. Do you know what it is?"

"Oh, aye, everybody does. That cave is as busy as Victoria Station since morning," Maria said. "He's not there. Now, if you'll please excuse me, gentlemen, I'd like to continue my reading. I can't help you." She turned away and continued to read.

The detectives felt out of place in the university library. Most students and faculty recognized them.

"I don't think there's anything here," Seamus whispered. "What do you think?"

"Don't get all rattled. We've plenty of time, settle down and let's see who makes the first move, a wee bit of quiet intimidation can't hurt anything."

Maguire pulled out his notebook and began to write. Seamus glanced around, wondering what it was like to do nothing all day except read.

Seamus with the restless eyes was first to notice the change in Maria's face. Her eyes, growing rounder, dug into the pages of her journal, scooping up the words. "Glory to be god…" she mumbled out loud. She hurried to the copy machine with the journal. She returned with a copy of an article stapled together which she placed in her brief case.

Maguire tried another tack. He said to her, "We've both been suspended without pay till we bring in Professor O'Donnell for questioning. That's going to work a hardship on our families. Will you help us a wee bit and ask O'Donnell to turn himself in? We'll see to it…"

"I'm sorry for your families," Maria said, "I really am, but I honestly don't know were Kevin O'Donnell is."

They believed her. Another dead end.

Maria got up and gathered her things. "Please excuse me, gentlemen," she said.

They watched her leave in silence. As soon as she had cleared the doorway, both dove for the journal she had been reading. Quickly Seamus found the flattened pages and read haltingly, 'Two Genetic Bases for Certain Aspects of the Human Immune System'. It's written by Karen Rolf of the University of Florida, a Yank. If there's anything here, it's beyond me." He tossed the journal onto the table.

Maguire picked it up and read the title and line or two of the abstract. He shrugged. "Isn't it strange?" he said. "Here's a woman who's deeply worried because her man is 'on the run' and she doesn't know where he is. Not only that, he has no place to go and no friends who'll offer him shelter. Yet she reads something in this magazine and immediately everything else is forgotten. Why?"

"Because she's a damn professor and it doesn't take much to set her off," Seamus said.

"Not on your life," Maguire said. He picked up the journal and carried it to the copier. He made himself a copy of the article, folded the sheets and put them into his pocket.

"What are you up to?" Seamus asked when Maguire returned to the table.

"There must be something in here connected with O'Donnell." He stared at the open journal. "Now what could it be?" He stood up. "We're going to fine out, so we'll stick to Miss Maria Burke like dog shit to her Wellingtons. Let's go."

11

The telephone repairman set his toolbox on the floor beside the secretary's desk and hunted through his pockets for a work order.

"Offices 211 through…" he began.

"Two-fourteen," the secretary finished, barely looking up from her stack of typing. "What's the problem?"

"One of the phones in here is causing radio interference on some of the equipment in this building. That's a big federal no-no. Has anyone complained about static or noise on the line?"

"Nope."

"Well, I guess I'll have to go through them one by one till I find the little rascal. How about unlocking the office doors?"

"That one's open," the secretary nodded her head toward the office directly opposite her. "I'll get the others."

She unlocked the doors and the repairman tried the phones in each office. He entered Karen Rolf's office last. He quickly detached her phone from the jack and stuffed it in his toolbox, replacing it with a similar piece of equipment.

When he completed the hook-up he walked to the window overlooking the bicycle shop across 13th Street.

"I've found it," he said in a normal speaking voice.

A bright light flashed twice from the doorway of the bicycle shop. The transmitting device was not functioning properly.

"What did you say?" the secretary called.

The repairman turned the phone over and twisted one of the base screws a quarter turn. He set the phone back on the desk and went to the window again.

"I said I found it," he repeated in a conversational tone. The light in the bicycle shop doorway flashed once. Good, they were receiving.

Quickly the repairman scooped up his tools, closed Karen's office door, and left.

"I couldn't hear what you were mumbling about back there," the secretary said without interrupting her typing.

"I was mostly talking to myself."

"Welcome to the club."

"Please tell whoever uses that office that I replaced the phone," the repairman said. "I'm pretty sure I got the right one." He walked to the door. "What are you doing for lunch?"

Without looking up the secretary replied, "Taking one of my kids to the dentist. Want to come?"

"Bye."

Early in the afternoon Julian Zeiss showed up unannounced in Karen's office suite. Karen's door was open. When she heard his voice she called to him and, bursting with enthusiasm, he hurried down the hallway.

Karen met him at the door. "What a nice surprise, Dr. Zeiss. I didn't expect…"

"I couldn't wait," he said, "I had to tell you that you may be on the track of the scientific discovery of the century. I'm so excited I don't know where to begin."

"Begin by plopping yourself in that chair."

Zeiss raved about her study and concluded with, "But you must have some actual, physical corroboration. The changes in blood protein which you noticed seem to indicate that other changes may have taken place in the skeletal structure. After all, the human body is a single piece of work. You need to collaborate with an anthropologist who can complement your work with supporting data."

"Yes?"

"And I'm your man!" Zeiss said. "How about it? It's a marvelous project. It's your idea, so your name would appear first on everything we publish."

Karen was about to say, 'It would, anyway; 'R' comes before 'Z'", but she wasn't about to dampen his enthusiasm. So she said, "I'm thrilled, Dr. Zeiss." After all, if he happened to be right, and with his reputation…

"Now there's one more thing I must tell you," Zeiss continued. "When I first read your paper I got so excited I faxed a copy to a colleague, an anthropologist, at Tel Aviv University."

"I'll send him all the copies he wants," Karen said.

"No, dear, that's not the problem. Good Zionist like he is, he evidently took the paper directly to the government, and the government turned it over to the Mossad."

"The Mossad?"

"The Israeli intelligence organization. They've already contacted me."

Zeiss told her of his phone call while the listeners in the bicycle shop across the street recorded every word.

When he finished, Karen said, "They've got some damn nerve! Do you think you ought to go to the police, or the F.B.I., or somebody in authority?"

"Lord, no. I'd just be caught in the middle of some international something or other."

"I really don't see what the Israelis have to do with this, it's my work, and this is an American university."

Zeiss said, "Think a moment about the Israeli situation. If the Arabs, or anyone else for that matter, could provide scientific evidence that they are intellectually superior to the Jews, they would gain a great propaganda victory."

"But it could turn out the other way, or the data might give no one an advantage."

"Ah, yes, but if you were an Israeli, surrounded on all sides by hostile neighbors, could you afford to sit back and wait for the data to fall? You understand why the Mossad must try to influence the outcome, don't you?"

"Well, how do we protect our work, and even ourselves?"

"We publish, get into print as quickly as possible," Zeiss said, "give the knowledge to the world and let world opinion protect us."

"I hope you're right. Dr. Zeiss, why are you telling me this? Why didn't you go along with the Mossad and simply discourage me from continuing? You might have saved yourself a lot of trouble."

"Don't think the idea didn't cross my mind. I'm a dyed-in-the-wool Zionist at heart. But...first, science is more important to me than any doctrine, even Zionism. And second—" he smiled broadly—"you are going to make us famous. Who is so humble that he can resist the lure of a Nobel prize?"

Karen smiled. "A Nobel prize? Do you think…"

"But we must move quickly," Zeiss urged. "Others will surely see the implications of your paper. Are we then to collaborate, you and I?"

"Okay, we're partners! Where do we begin?"

"Tonight I'll work out a protocol for myself," Zeiss said, "and you do the same. We'll get together…when?"

"How about tomorrow evening, say, seven, in my office?"

"Good," Zeiss agreed, "and we'll review and combine the best of both into a good workable schedule." He stood up. "I haven't been this excited about anything since my first dig. We'll make a great team, beauty and the beast, so to speak."

Later in the afternoon Zeiss tried to take his usual nap but his mind was racing. Where to begin? He rose and put on his jacket. "Going for a walk," he called to his wife.

As he passed the vacant donut shop on N.E. 8th Street, a small thin man stepped out of the alley leading to the back entrance of the shop. He blocked Zeiss' way.

"Excuse me" Zeiss said and tried to walk around him.

"Are you Julian Zeiss, Sol Braverman's friend?" the little man asked.

Zeiss stopped. "I am. Who are you?" The voice sounded familiar.

"I have a message from Sol," the man replied in a carefully articulated Jewish accent. "Can we get off this public street?"

He walked down the alley and Zeiss followed, looking around.

"I have a message on tape for you from Sol," the man said, walking to his parked car and retrieving a small tape recorder. "I'm sure you'll be able to recognize his voice."

"He turned on the recorder.

"Julian, my friend…" It was Sol all right but his voice sounded as though it had been taped off the phone. "…please take the Rolf affair very, very seriously. For your own safety, and lovely Becky's, do as they want. Julian, do you understand? You are in grave danger. Please tell this man you'll work with the Mossad. Please, Julian."

The little man shut off the recorder, looked at Zeiss and said, "Do you have a message for Sol?"

"Yes," Zeiss said, "tell him I thank him for his concern, but tell him I'm an American citizen, an American scientist, and I intend to follow my work, wherever it leads me."

"Is that all?"

"That's all."

Suddenly, there in the deserted alley, Zeiss was looking down the barrel of a long black silencer on the end of a handgun.

"Kneel down, please," the little man ordered.

"I will not," Zeiss replied, close to panic.

The silencer was rammed into Zeiss' chest, hard, directly over his heart. "Last time, kneel down please, the man said.

With difficulty, Zeiss lowered himself to the rough pavement in a kneeling position.

"Are you certain you have no other message for Sol?" the man asked, raising the gun to Zeiss' forehead.

"You can't intimidate me, you son-of-a-bitch..."

The gun popped quietly and a gaping hole suddenly burst open in the middle of Zeiss' forehead. He fell over on his side.

The little man quickly put the gun in his pocket and pulled on a pair of latex gloves. He tore the cover from a condom and pressed the condom into Zeiss' still-twitching fingers. Next he reached down and unzipped the fly of Zeiss' trousers. He reached inside and roughly exposed Zeiss' penis. He emptied the trouser pockets over the ground and finally took Zeiss' wallet. He looked around, double checking his work. Finally he pumped one more shot into the side of Zeiss' head, climbed into his car and drove out of the alley.

About an hour later a youngster skateboarding in the alley discovered the body.

A stunned Karen Rolf heard of Zeiss' murder on the evening news. Just enough details and innuendo were supplied to hint at a minor scandal involving a university professor. Even in her sorrow, Becky Zeiss didn't believe it, and neither did Karen Rolf.

After the initial shock, Karen began to think of her own personal papers and detailed plans that she had worked on that afternoon and left in her office. They might be safer at home. "David, will you ride with me to the office while I get some paperwork I forgot?" she asked her husband.

"Sorry, honey, I have a meeting."

You bastard, every time I need you...

"The campus is well lit," he added, "plenty of people walking around, good security."

"Yes, of course," she said. "I just thought you might like the ride."

"Sorry."

When Karen drove into the deserted parking lot she was relieved to see the lights blazing in the bicycle shop across the street.

The medical center buzzed with night-time activity—lab experiments hummed, tired-looking graduate students walked the hallways, medical students locked themselves in the gross anatomy lab. She let herself into her office just as the phone on the front desk jangled loudly. She hesitated; the office was closed till morning. Still the phone rang insistently, urgently. She picked up the receiver.

"Department of Microbiology. Karen Rolf speaking."

Pause. Static crackling. Then, Oh, thank goodness it's you, Professor Rolf. I thought I'd never reach you at this hour but it was worth a try."

"Who is this, please?"

"My name is Maria Burke, I'm a psychologist, and I'm calling from the University of Northern Ireland."

"Where?"

"Northern Ireland, just outside of Londonderry. It's one o'clock in the morning here, but this can't wait."

They talked for almost an hour. When Karen finally left the office, the lights in the bicycle shop still burned brightly. They burned throughout the night, long after Karen's offer to hire Irish anthropologist Dr. Kevin O'Donnell had leaped via satellite to Israel.

12

"I'm Maria Burke." She faced the tall bearded man in the doorway and knew him instantly. "Sorry to get you up so early."

He smiled and the guarded suspicion vanished. He looked around behind her into the early morning drizzle. "Are you alone?" he asked.

"Aye."

His quick eyes caught the silent gliding of a car to the curb a few blocks away.

"Well, you're not, but no matter. Come in, Maria. I would know you anywhere from Kevin's rantin' and ravin'." Barry O'Donnell closed the door behind her.

"Och, Kevin exaggerates a wee bit, doesn't he?"

Barry looked her over. "Not this time," he said.

"Barry, I need a favor. Kevin's in bad trouble. Will you help me find him and get him on a plane to America?" Maria asked.

"Och, now, wait a minute." Barry rubbed his eyes. "For god's sake, why?"

She told him the whole story, including her conversation with Karen Rolf and the offer to hire Kevin at the University of Florida. When she finished, Barry got up and poured them both a cup of tea.

"Now isn't that just like bloody Kevin," he said, "stirring up a hornet's nest over nothing at all?"

Maria raised her eyebrows. "Nothing to you, maybe…"

"Och, go on, Maria, I know what Kevin's been doing. The police have been here already, and I've made a few inquiries of my own."

"Well, then…"

"If Kevin's going to play games with the authorities, then he has to learn when to fold and take his losses."

"Not Kevin. He doesn't fold."

"Well, then, he's a bloody fool and that's why he's in trouble and why the police are following you," Barry said.

"Will you help me find him?"

Barry signed. "I think I know where he is."

"Where?"

"Never mind that. You're being followed, your phone's probably tapped, and you shouldn't be here. I want you to go back to the university and stay there till you hear from me."

"Will you ring me soon? It must be soon."

"Aye." He urged her to the door. "Be off with you and take your watch dogs with you. Someone will get in touch with you soon. Do exactly what they tell you. Do you understand?"

"Aye, I do."

"And do you understand that the both of you are dealing with dangerous people?"

"I've suspected that," Maria said, "but sometimes I wonder if Kevin does."

Barry shook his head. "Jesus," he muttered.

"What did I tell you?" Maguire said, nudging Seamus. "Follow her and we'll nab his nibs in short order." They watched Maria leave Barry O'Donnell's house and climb into her car.

"What about him?" Seamus asked, jerking his head toward Barry's house. "Someone ought to keep an eye on him."

"Don't worry about him. He can't go for a jar without the Brits or the police following him. Besides, even if he knows where his brother is, he's too damn fly to lead us to him. Now start the car and don't let her get too far ahead of us."

They tailed Maria's car down the Donegal Road and onto the M1 motorway.

"Are we going back to the university?" Seamus asked, fiddling with the broken heater.

"Forget that goddamn heater!" Maguire snapped. "It doesn't work. You'll run us up a pole if you don't watch where you're going. No, we're not going to the university. We stick out like shit up an entry in that place."

"How are we going to keep tabs on the Burke woman?"

"I wish you'd shift your brains into gear and do some thinking for yourself," Maguire complained.

For answer, Seamus slammed on the brakes and almost hurled Maguire through the windshield. "And that's about all the shit I'm going to take from you," he shouted. He stopped the car dead in the middle of the motorway. Horns blew all around them. "If you can't keep a civil tongue…"

"All right, for christssake, I didn't mean it," Maguire said, eyeing the traffic. "This business has me up the wall. I'm sorry, Seamus. Move us before we have a four-ton Mitsubishi up our tail pipe."

Seamus sulked. "Don't go taking your frustration out on me," he said, slowly driving off. "I want the bastard as much as you do. You were supposed to watch the back door of the professor's digs, weren't you, and you went off nicking fish and chips, didn't you? If you'd been doing your job, we'd have him now."

"I said I'm sorry, Seamus. I've made arrangements for people at the university to watch Maria Burke for us, students in her classes. Anything new or unusual, where she goes, when she leaves—we'll know it all. She'll even be followed into the bloody loo, and we'll know if she does Number One or Number Two. We'll know everything. All we have to do is sit by the phone in the station and wait for the calls to come in."

Seamus was impressed. "How did you manage that?"

"A bit of persuasion, intimidation…"

"And maybe a fiver here and there, huh?"

"Whatever works."

When Maria Burke's class in Abnormal Psychology met at one-o'clock, there was one strange face in the crowd. Maria ignored the stranger, a woman in her early twenties. The usual comments and questions followed the lecture and Maria soon forgot about the stranger until the class ended. When the others filed out, the stranger approached Maria.

"Can we talk here?" she asked.

Maria noticed that one of her regular students was still lingering over her books in the rear of the room.

"Did you wish to see me, Rose?" Maria called.

"No, m'am. I'm working on tomorrow's assignment. Am I in the way?"

"No, not at all." Maria and the stranger walked to the door.

"Who was that?" the stranger asked.

"Och, just a student. I've known her for two years."

The woman lowered her voice. "Barry says to pick up a small suitcase for Kevin in Coleraine, just a small one, mind you. Get a tooth brush and shirt, underwear, you know, the usual stuff. Then you're to drive to Armagh."

"Armagh?"

"Aye, and hurry. There's no time. I'll follow in my car. We'll leave my car for Kevin, and you can drive me back to Coleraine."

"Will I see Kevin?"

"Maybe for a minute or two. We have to go now. I'll be behind you in the blue Fiesta. We'll stop at McSorley's pub in Armagh and I'll give you more directions. All right?"

Maria nodded and hurried out of the building. The stranger followed her.

The Chief Constable eyed both of them suspiciously. "You're not thinking you'll be weaslin' your way back on duty, are you?"

"Och, no, Chief," Maguire said, "we're on to something and we need a table and a phone, somewhere out of the way…"

"To do what?"

Maguire looked at Seamus, who said, "It's a bit ticklish, Chief, what with one of our own…"

"Do you have a tail on Maria Burke?"

"Aye," Maguire answered, "more or less."

"Use the weapons room," the Chief said, "and run in a phone line. I don't want either of you underfoot until you bring me O'Donnell. Understand?"

Maguire and Seamus moved in immediately, in shirt sleeves, with a pot of tea and a telephone. "It will be a long day," Maguire said, "but worth it, you'll see."

The phone rang. "Action already," Maguire said, grabbing the telephone.

He listened for a few minutes then said, "Good job. You come on back and Clare will take over." He hung up the phone.

"Burke's buying a case and some clothes in Colleraine," Maguire said. "She's being followed by a woman in a blue Ford Fiesta with Belfast license plates. What do you think?"

Seamus' eyes darted about the small weapons room. "Seems too simple, doesn't it?"

"What do you mean?"

"Well, her buying clothes and all in plain daylight."

"Maybe," Maguire answered, "but don't forget, there's no police in sight. Her own students are following her, and they're changed regularly. The woman in the Fiesta's probably I.R.A., and she'll be looking for police, not students."

Seamus nodded. Seemed logical.

The phone rang again and Maguire scribbled a few notes on a pad. He hung up the receiver. "They're driving south out of Coleraine on Highway 29," he said. He unfolded a map and spread it on the table. "Where do you think they're going, Seamus?"

Seamus studied the map. "Across the border at Monaghan or Newry, take your pick. Me, I'd have Newry and get lost in the truck traffic."

"But first they have to get O'Donnell."

"Maybe," Seamus replied, "or leave him one of the cars."

"So they'll stay together, at least until they find him. Is that what you're thinking?" Maguire asked.

"Aye, but it still seems too simple, doesn't it?"

"Not if you're desperate and trying to get someone across the border."

An uneventful hour passed, then a knock at the door and Phil Burke entered.

"Are you having any luck?" he asked.

Seamus looked at Maguire, and both of them seemed embarrassed.

"Ah, well…" Maguire began.

"I know all about it," Phil said. "Chief told me everything. Where is my sister?"

"About an hour south of Coleraine," Seamus answered.

"Is she in any danger?" Phil asked.

"I shouldn't think so," Maguire said. "But she's got company, I.R.A. more than likely, following in a Belfast car. And the Coleraine police behind the both of them."

Phil looked at the map spread on the table. Seamus and Maguire were obviously uneasy in his presence.

"No shooting," Phil said, "I don't want her put in harm's way."

Maguire shrugged. "We're not there," he said. "Coleraine's in charge."

Phil pointed to the phone. "Tell them no shooting," he said, and his sudden tone of voice set Seamus' eyes blinking and darting about the room.

"Aye, Phil." Maguire picked up the phone.

A short time later Phil left. Seamus and Maguire gulped lukewarm tea, and Seamus paced the small room, glancing frequently at the phone. Time passed slowly. Finally Maguire said, "For christssake, Seamus, sit down, or go take a piss or something."

The one small barred window in the weapons room was darkening noticeably when the phone rang.

The voice on the other end said, "They've stopped in Armagh, at a pub called McSorley's."

"Armagh?" Maguire's finger found it on the map. "What are they doing?"

"They're sitting in a booth having a sandwich and a cup of tea. Did you find out anything about the Fiesta?"

"It's clean," Maguire said. "Seamus thinks they may try to cross at Monaghan or Newry. What do you think?"

A few seconds of silence. "I think they're waiting for someone. They're taking their sweet time and the Burke woman seems a wee bit nervous."

Maguire nodded and said, "Of course, of course." He smiled confidently at Seamus. "Stay out of sight and watch the back door," he told the caller. "I want to know the minute something happens. If O'Donnell shows, take him into custody immediately. Use all the force you need.

He hung up the receiver and rubbed his hands together. "Well, now, we may be on to something. Warm up the tea and put a smile on that glum kisser of yours." He winked at Seamus. "The professor is as good as in the bag."

Seamus managed a wan smile. "Maybe."

"Jesus, you're hopeless. Doom and gloom, himself."

The afternoon light in the tiny barred window slipped away. Seamus sat watching the phone and now Maguire paced the room like a caged bear.

At five o'clock the phone rang.

Maguire dove for the instrument and snapped a brusque hello into the speaker. He listened for a minute or two then hung up the receiver without saying a word. Seamus watched anxiously, blinking wildly.

Maguire picked up his tea mug and hurled it against the wall. "Bastard!" he raged, his voice quiet, furious. Fascinated, Seamus watched the tea dregs slither down the freshly painted wall.

13

One street light fanned yellowish rays into the gloom, casting dancing shadows on the deserted sea wall. Lights glowed in the windows of the elegantly-aged apartment houses ringing the Portrush promenade and a steady drizzle, soft as a snowfall, fell on the peninsula. The calm, black sea flowed into the night sky along the far horizon.

Barry O'Donnell sat on the sea wall looking across the water, waiting for Maria Burke to speak.

She said, at last, "And where would he be about now?"

Barry glanced at his wrist watch. Eight-thirty. "Oh, about half way to New York."

"I wanted a minute with him, only a minute," she said, and the street light gleamed in eyes glistening with tears.

"I know," Barry said, "but it was hopeless. I knew you would be followed all day by the police. I counted on it."

She nodded her head. "Aye. Still…"

A long silence full of unsaid farewells. A dark, drizzly night. Cold.

"Did he leave a message for me?" she asked.

"He said he loved you, he would be back, he said he would call and write. He felt worse than you. You know Kevin."

She cried softly into a wet handkerchief.

"Aren't you curious how I managed to get him on a plane to New York?" Barry asked, more to break the awkward spell.

"You're Barry, aren't you. And hasn't Kevin told me Barry could do anything?" Her voice was quiet and full of crying when she spoke.

Encouraged, Barry continued. "He was in the cave beneath Dunluce." He smiled, remembering the welcoming hugs when he found Kevin, cold and hungry, sitting on the ledge at the base of the cliff trying to fish with a strap from his knapsack. "We drove to Knock."

"To Knock? I should've guessed."

"To the airport where the American charter planes land for the Shrine."

"How did you know when a plane would be leaving?"

"I belong to a knowledgeable organization. Anyway, we had a back-up at Cork."

"I still don't see how you got him on a charter plane."

"I convinced a cooperative American pilgrim that Our Lady of Knock would appreciate his seat for an Irishman in trouble."

"How did you manage to get away from the Belfast police?" she asked.

He was glad to hear the genuine curiosity in her voice. He had managed to take her mind off Kevin for a moment at least.

"Can you keep a secret?" he asked.

She hesitated. "I'm not sure I want to know secrets. Secrets carry an awful burden of trust," she said.

"I trust anyone that Kevin loves."

"Then tell me. How did you get away from the police and drive from Belfast to Dunluce?"

For the first time that night he looked at her, into her eyes, and she looked back. She saw the same strength and determination she had often sensed in her brother, Phil.

"There's more than one me," he whispered. "I sent one of me to Bangor, in the opposite direction, and took the police for a ride down the Ards."

"Just like I took them to Armagh?"

"Aye."

"And those other 'you's…?"

"Och, no more. Kevin's safe for the moment and on his way, and wasn't that what you asked me to do?"

She leaned over and kissed him on the cheek, just above the drizzle-soaked beard. "Aye. Kevin was right. You are a remarkable man."

"Och, we'll see, it's not over yet, is it?" Barry said. He rose, and then he was off, gone, blending into the shadows of the promenade.

Maria hurried home to phone Karen Rolf that Kevin was on his way.

14

His code name was Joseph Hecht. His real name was buried deep within the records of the Mossad. He was fifty-five years old, Brooklyn-born (Eastern Parkway), and he had never set foot in Israel.

When his father died he inherited the family bookstore on Staten Island which he and his father had managed. He was a small frail man, a bachelor, no family except for a distant cousin who lived somewhere in Arizona. He was also a passionate Zionist. On a whim, he wrote a letter to the Israeli government offering his services as an expert on rare books and documents. He heard nothing for six months and then a Mossad agent called at the bookstore.

The agent must have sensed something special about Hecht, for a clerk was hired for the bookstore and Hecht was sent to Long Island for two weeks of training in firearms and explosives.

The agent's instincts were true. Joseph Hecht possessed the mind of a political assassin, he asked no questions, sought no reward, felt no remorse, and he was surprisingly innovative. Best of all, he looked like anyone's grandfather, unobtrusive, ordinary, the perfect mole.

His first assignment came within the year, the termination of a Syrian-born Jew who turned out vicious anti-Semitic propaganda from a small print shop near Waukegan, Illinois. Hecht burned the shop to the ground. The authorities found the badly charred remains of the Syrian inside a small toilet facility which, for some inexplicable reason, had been locked from the outside.

The Mossad was pleased and deposited one hundred thousand dollars in a Bronx bank to cover the cost of future ops. Until he was assigned to the Rolf matter, Hecht had successfully completed fourteen missions for the Mossad without a hitch. By now, the C.I.A. were reasonably certain that a Mossad professional was operating somewhere out of the east coast but were unable to trace him through the usual sources.

The secret of Hecht's success was his eerie ability to remain unnoticed. When in service, he always carried a package of some sort which partially obscured his features, so he looked like one of hundreds of other people scurrying about their business. Witnesses were never sure if they actually saw him, and those who claimed to, varied wildly in their descriptions. Joseph Hecht entered quietly, did his work, and disappeared, and always left behind the possibility of accident, doubt, or coincidence. His work had earned him respect deep within the Mossad which used him now only for high priority ops.

Hecht tackled the Rolf matter in his usual precise and impersonal style. Having eliminated Zeiss, he was then ordered to intercept and terminate Kevin O'Donnell. As far as Hecht was concerned the assignment was routine until he received a careful briefing on O'Donnell's background, including the reason for his current difficulties with the Mossad and the government of Northern Ireland. As a literate man, Hecht took a personal interest in the case and learned as much as he could about O'Donnell's work.

O'Donnell became not only an enemy of the Israeli state, but Hecht's own personal foe, a dangerous man with a dangerous idea that could upset world affairs.

Hecht reasoned that a fugitive from Northern Ireland or the Irish Republic would hardly flee the country aboard a national carrier or even on a scheduled airliner. Hecht's plan was to meet the charter flights and catch O'Donnell in New York before he reached Gainesville.

An intercepted telephone conversation between Maria Burke in Northern Ireland and Dr. Rolf in Gainesville confirmed Hecht's hunch. Kevin O'Donnell had indeed left Ireland aboard an Access charter flight from Knock, Ireland, bound for Kennedy Airport in New York. After two scheduled stops on the continent, the plane would arrive in New York about 6:00 A.M.. Perfect. O'Donnell would be tired, sleepy and grateful for any assistance.

Ordinarily Hecht would have rented a car, using a stolen credit card. However, rental offices were closed for the night, and he was in a hurry. He stole a late model car from his own Brooklyn neighborhood and drove to the bookstore on Staten Island. Hecht was a methodical man who hated to be rushed. He washed up in a back room of the store, sat down with the evening paper, and waited. He dozed off a few times during the late evening but at three o'clock in the morning he drove off on schedule.

He arrived at Kennedy before the morning traffic and finally located the terminal and gate were the Access charter was scheduled to disembark. Although the clocks in the terminal showed 5:00 A.M., relatives and friends were gathering in the lounge behind customs. Hecht slipped among them unnoticed and sat down. A flashing sign reported that Access flight 1103 would arrive one hour late.

Hecht had not formulated a specific plan because he had discovered that his on-the-spot improvisations were frequently better than his plans. The stolen car posed a problem since it could be traced back to his Eastern Parkway neighborhood. He had to get rid of both O'Donnell and the car.

He pulled out a road map of the Eastern U.S. and mentally traced a route southward. By avoiding the Interstate highways he was certain that many opportunities would arise along the way. He had confidence in his own ability to seize the moment and never doubted for an instant that O'Donnell and the car would vanish before next morning.

Access flight 1103 arrived in a jostling, noise mass of people pushing and shoving through customs, calling to friends, babies crying, a throng of sleepy-eyed, tousle-haired humanity, laughing and hugging, stacks of luggage everywhere…

In the middle of it all, wide-eyed, rumpled, without luggage, Kevin O'Donnell…

"Are you Dr. O'Donnell?" Hecht asked, smiling reassuringly.

A great sigh of relief. "Aye, I'm O'Donnell."

Hecht shook his hand. "I'm Joseph Levy. Dr. Rolf sent me to meet you."

"Great! You work with Dr. Rolf?"

"Same university but not the same college. I'm a librarian pressed into service because I just happened to be driving back to Gainesville."

"We're not flying?"

"No. Dr. Rolf didn't think it would be safe to fly into Gainesville. The airport's small and easily watched. My car's outside."

"How in the world did Dr. Rolf manage to plan all this on such short notice?" Kevin asked.

Hecht laughed. "Wait till you meet Dr. Rolf and you'll know. She's a dynamo. But actually, Dr. Burke from Coleraine phoned last night and told her when and where you would arrive."

"Ah," said Kevin, "I see." Always Maria smoothing the way. "Well, okay, let's go before someone decides to take another look at my passport."

"Do you have luggage?"

"I'm wearing it except for…" Kevin held up the bodhran.

"A drum?" Hecht asked, curious.

"A bodhran, a kind of drum."

Hecht raised his eyebrows. "Well, to each his own. Dr. Rolf will make arrangements for you when we reach Gainesville. Are you ready?"

"Aye," Kevin replied.

"Follow me," Hecht said and pushed through the crowd.

What was there about this man that disturbed Kevin? His voice? The careful way he avoided people? The newspaper he used to obscure his face? The New York license plates on a car from Florida?

Kevin climbed into the car but his Falls Road instincts sensed…danger?

93

15

David Rolf knew his wife wanted to say something from the way she poured his coffee and set the breakfast table. Ordinarily they spoke little at breakfast. He waited.

"I've invited a new faculty member to share the guest room for a few days," Karen began, "maybe a week or so until we can find him an apartment."

"Who is 'We'?"

"You know, the department. Do you have any objections?"

Silence. "Who is this guy?" David asked, buttering his toast. "It is a guy?"

"An anthropologist from Ireland."

"A what? What's he doing here?"

"It's a long story," Karen said.

"Then don't tell me." Silence. "Is he young or old?"

"David, you make me furious. I'm trying to hold an intelligent conversation with you, and you're turning it into an inquisition."

"Ah, I've struck a nerve. He's a young guy. I thought we had agreed that the house was off limits…"

"You're a fine damn one to talk, aren't you?" Karen said. "This is business, David, strictly business, and I expect you to be civil."

"Just like you were civil," David said.

"I apologized and paid for the damage to the car, didn't I?"

You're capable of anything. "What do you want from me?"

"Common courtesy. He's a house guest and an colleague."

"Screw him."

"If we can't agree on such a small thing, especially to a foreigner who knows nothing about our problems and expects to be made welcome, then I'll find a motel for him, but I'll remember how uncooperative you were."

Silence. David had experienced Karen's long memory and figured it was time to back off.

"Suit yourself," he said, "you know that blackmail works every time with me. He's your guest and your problem. I intend to be my usual forthright self, so warn him not to expect too much from me. And I'd like him out of the house in a reasonable time."

They both lapsed into silence.

David asked, "What the hell are you working on, anyway? I've never seen you so jumpy and nervous."

Karen almost burst into tears, but she didn't. The murder of Professor Zeiss had unnerved her.

"Stress, I guess," she replied. "Classes, committee meetings, grant deadlines, you know."

David glanced across the table at her. "You've been doing that for years and it hasn't bothered you. This is different, isn't it?"

Karen hesitated. "Yes, it is."

"In what way?"

"I'm not prepared to talk about it now, David. Believe me, it's all part of work. Nothing more."

He wasn't convinced. "Are you in some kind of trouble?" he asked.

Karen got up, dumped her coffee into the sink and left the kitchen.

Munching thoughtfully on his toast, David watched her go. What the hell? What's going on here, anyway?

16

A few miles north of Rocky Mount, North Carolina, Kevin dozed in the passenger seat while Hecht scanned the road ahead in search of a suitable place to get rid of car and passenger. The sun had set and a soft twilight lingered over the lightly-traveled highway.

Earlier in the afternoon when they had stopped for a hamburger and Kevin had gone to the rest room, Hecht had taped a powerful incendiary explosive under the driver's seat and wired it to a radio-controlled detonator. With the transmitter in his pocket, he had only to find a way to persuade Kevin to drive off alone. Hecht knew from experience that with a full tank of fuel, the explosion and fire would destroy car and passenger beyond recognition. The best time would be just after dark, south of Rocky Mount, when traffic would be light and he was still close enough to walk back to town. A taxi to the bus station, and once again Hecht would slip out of town unnoticed. He had done it before, he couldn't fail. The Mossad had supplied him with the most powerful devices in the world.

"Are you awake?" Hecht asked Kevin.

"Aye," Kevin replied.

"The car seems to be pulling to the left when I brake," Hecht said, "we may have to check the brake fluid."

"Is it bad?"

"Bad enough. When we stop for gas, you drive and I'll stand alongside the road and see if I notice anything unusual."

Kevin was wide awake now, and puzzled. "Let's just stop at the next garage and check the brake fluid." He glanced at the fuel gauge. "We need gas, anyway."

"Too much traffic here, Hecht answered. "It will only take a minute when we're south of town. I want you to try it. Maybe it's must my imagination."

Kevin shrugged. "Okay, but it's getting so dark I'm wondering what you'll be able to see."

What bloody nonsense, thought Kevin. Too much traffic? He hadn't seen another car in minutes. And how can he check anything standing outside on a dark road? Wasn't he the queer one, though? He hadn't spoken a word in hours. Certainly not like the librarians I've known; they'd talk the horns of a goat. The more Kevin thought about the strange Mr. Levy, the more he wondered. And didn't he show up at the airport at just the right time, too? A librarian? Well, let's find out, Mr. Levy.

"I have a few friends who are librarians," Kevin said. "Which library do you work in?"

"The University of Florida. I told you."

"No, I mean, which branch, medical, education, science…"

Hecht hesitated. "Main library."

"And your specialty is?"

"Rare books and documents. Why do you ask?"

"Just interested. You're sort of an archivist, then?"

Hecht's annoyance was beginning to show. "I work in the archives, yes."

Okay, thought Kevin, that's a start. "You have the Marjorie Kinnan Rawlings collection at the University of Florida, don't you? I hope I get a chance to browse through it."

"I'll arrange it," Hecht said. "A new Rawlings manuscript surfaced up here in the Carolinas—Blood of My Blood. Did you know about that?"

"Aye. I also understand James Joyce is still popular in the States. Do you have any first editions?"

Hecht slowed the car. This Irisher son-of-a-bitch is actually testing me. Well, he picked the wrong person and the wrong subject.

"We have nothing like the Dublin manuscript at Yale University," Hecht said, "but I have a Huebsch first U.S. edition in my own private collection."

"Do you now!" exclaimed Kevin. "That was 1918, wasn't it?"

Barely containing his annoyance. "No, 1916." You son-of-a-bitch. "I didn't think anthropologists kept up with such things."

"Irish ones do. In fact, I own a Grant Richards first edition of The Dubliners."

"London, 1914," Hecht said.

"Bravo," Kevin said, "you know your Joyce."

"I know the archives," Hecht answered, "why did you doubt it?"

"Och, it's my Northern Irish suspicion," Kevin said. "In my country you learn to trust nobody. Sorry, Mr. Levy, no offense meant."

"Oh, that's all right." I underestimated you, you bastard, you could be dangerous. Hecht saw a lighted convenience store sign a few blocks ahead and quickly made up his mind. We'll take care of that right now.

"You're right, we're low on gas. I'm going to pull in ahead and fill up."

Hecht parked the car at the rear pump, out of sight of the store clerk. "My wallet's in the attache case on the rear seat," he said, "please reach back and hand the case to me."

Hecht climbed out of the car and filled up the tank, carefully staying in the shadows. When he finished, he gave Kevin a twenty-dollar bill.

"Here, would you mind paying the clerk inside?. When you come back, I want you to drive the car a mile or so and see if it pulls to the left. I'll wait here for you."

"Okay." Kevin took the money and entered the store. He returned a few minutes later followed closely by a tall lanky youth in a baseball cap. Only when they were inches away did Hecht see the gun in Kevin's back. The youth quickly turned the gun on Hecht.

"Put your attache case on the trunk of the car and open it," he demanded.

"Do as he says, Mr. Levy," Kevin said, "he just shot the clerk inside."

"That's right, and you're next, old man, if you don't move your ass. Open the case."

Hecht fumbled with the latch and finally raised the lid of the attache case. Lying on top of a few articles of clothing was a heavy black pistol with a long black silencer.

"Holy shit!" the youth exclaimed. "You've got a bigger piece than I do." He quickly grabbed the pistol and a box of shells. "What are you—some kind of cop?"

"No," Hecht replied, "that's for self protection."

"My ass," the youth replied, "you're some kind of fed. You look like one. Empty your pockets into the case. You, too," he pushed the gun into Kevin's back. "Hurry up. If a car pulls in here I'll waste the both of you."

Kevin and Hecht tossed their wallets, keys, and watches into the attache case. "What's that sticking out of your pocket?" the youth asked Hecht.

Hecht showed him the transmitter which was about the size of a pocket calculator. A telescoping antenna jutted out from one corner. "It's the regulator for my heart pacer," Hecht said.

"Toss it in the case."

"I need it," Hecht insisted. "I could die without it. It's no use to you."

The youth examined the transmitter then tossed it back to Hecht. "Okay, old man, take off. Run. If you stop or look back till we're out of here, I'll shoot you in the back."

Hecht shuffled into the shadows behind the store.

The gunman pointed his weapon at Kevin. "I need a hostage; you drive." He slammed the lid of Hecht's attache case and tossed it into the car. He climbed into the passenger seat beside Kevin and shoved the gun into Kevin's ribs. "Turn left, slowly, and stay within the speed limit. We're going north."

Squatting in the dark behind crates of trash in back of the store, Hecht watched the car drive away. He could scarcely believe his good fortune. The car was headed north along an empty road. He couldn't have planned it better.

Quickly he extended the antenna and armed the transmitter which responded with a blinking red light. He would wait about three minutes and push the firing button. Perfect. He pointed the antenna in the direction of the retreating car.

17

Maria tried to concentrate but her mind wasn't on the article in her hands. She read and re-read portions, tried to focus her attention only to have her thoughts wander to the strange group of people with whom she shared the outer waiting room of the chancellor's office.

She glanced at Brian McKensie, nervous as a schoolboy summoned to the headmaster's office. His eyes momentarily caught hers and he tried to smile, weakly, but the result made him seem even more uncomfortable.

Seamus and Maguire were another matter. They waited with the patience of policemen, bored and unimpressed. Both wore shapeless dark suits, grey-white wrinkled shirts and dark ties. Maguire thumbed through his ever-present notebook, a cheap pocket-size pad held together by a spiral binding. He jabbed and jotted with a ballpoint pen, breathing heavily through is mouth, oblivious to everything except his own need to record the special things that seemed important to him.

Seamus' eyes stared at Maria's legs, not a lustful stare, but rather a thoughtful appraisal. He followed the flowing curves of the ankles to the long, slim calves, even higher, until the legs disappeared within the mysterious folds of Maria's skirt. Seamus sighed audibly and the others glanced over at him. Unembarrassed, he smiled and nodded appreciatively at Maria. She returned his smile, locked her legs tightly together, and went back to her reading. Rain hammered the window panes of the outer office, and the receptionist, seated at her tidy desk near the door, drew the sweater draped across her shoulders tightly about her. Everyone waited.

About ten minutes later the door to an inner office opened and the chancellor's personal secretary appeared.

"Please come this way," she said.

The group entered a conference room dominated by a rectangular table that occupied most of the central floor. The secretary indicated the dark brown leather chairs arranged around the table and said, "Please be seated. His Grace will join you shortly."

The secretary seated herself at the bottom of the table and everyone found seats along the sides. Except Seamus. He deliberately sat in the chancellor's seat at the head of the table and folded his arms, casually looking around the room.

McKensie and Maguire were horrified. Maguire desperately tried to catch Seamus' eye, but Seamus seemed to look every way except in Maguire's direction. Finally the secretary tiptoed to the front of the table and whispered something in Seamus' ear. Feigning surprise, Seamus' eyes blinked wildly. He said, "Sorry," smiled at everyone, gave up the head seat, and found a chair next to Maria.

He settled back and gently poked Maria with his elbow. "Seat's taken," he said in a booming whisper, "but if His Worship doesn't show soon, I'm for starting without him. What about you?"

Maria tried to be serious, considering the gravity of the situation, but couldn't help smiling. "You're daft," she whispered.

Maguire glanced apprehensively at McKensie, and both looked helplessly at the secretary who busied herself in her own note pad and appeared not to notice any of them.

Late afternoon clung like a grey film to the windows as the wind and rain rattled the panes. An expectant silence settled over the room. Seamus fidgeted, Maguire and McKensie could hardly take their eyes off the door to the inner office, and Maria grew more angry by the minute at this deliberate waste of her time.

Eventually the door to the inner office opened and the chancellor himself appeared, a ruddy-complexioned man, middle-aged, tall and heavy-set. He wore a dark blue suit, a starched white shirt set off with a reddish paisley tie. He sat down heavily at the head of the table.

"Good afternoon, ladies and gentlemen," he said, setting a manila folder on the table and leaning back in his chair. He glanced around the table and seeing Maria for the first time was clearly struck by her exceptional features. She was not what he had expected. Prior to the meeting, he had glanced through her personnel file and had made up his mind that she would be the typical academic. Her striking blue eyes, however, and shy, disarming smile took him completely by surprise.

"Professor Burke," he began, addressing Maria, "the police, represented here by these gentlemen, have brought some serious accusations against you. They claim that you aided a fugitive to flee the country, a suspected I.R.A. terrorist wanted by the police. That, of course, is a criminal charge that has no bearing on the substance of this hearing, which is to offer you the opportunity to tell your side of the story, and to justify your actions to the university. I should tell you, however, if you fail to do so to my satisfaction, I shall seek your dismissal through the Board of Trustees. The police may then file formal criminal charges against you. And, off the record—", he glanced at his secretary who looked up and stopped writing, "a good loyalist judge and jury could send you away for a few years."

Maria, who had been listening attentively, said, "In that case, Your Grace, considering the seriousness of the charges, I think I should be represented by counsel. If this is a formal hearing, then I request a postponement until I can obtain legal representation."

That was not at all what the chancellor wanted to hear. He knew there was scant legal merit to his charges, and, for that matter, to the accusations of the police. He had merely wished to set a climate of intimidation in which Maria might be inclined to cooperate. On the other hand, the charges weren't without some foundation. Even the suspicion of felony might be sufficient to bring her activity to the attention of the Board. He was confident he could have her job if he so wished. Nevertheless, he decided to pursue a different line of persuasion.

"My choice of words was perhaps confusing," the chancellor said. "This is not a formal hearing and no action will be taken as a result of it." He smiled. "So please excuse my preliminary remarks if they alarmed you, Dr. Burke."

He turned to the policemen. "That being the case, gentlemen, unless you have anything more to add to what you've already told me, you are excused." He dismissed them with a flip of his hand. "The rest of the meeting is for—ah—university business."

Maguire stood immediately, confused, but eager to be off. "Good day, Your Grace," he said.

Seamus rose a little slower. Maguire caught his eye and shot him an unspoken plea to keep his mouth shut. Seamus hesitated, then followed Maguire to the door.

"By the way," the chancellor addressed the departing police, "I've already spoken to your superior, and you have been reinstated—with pay."

"Thank you, Your Grace," Maguire said.

Even Seamus managed a mumbled thanks, then they left the room, closing the door softly behind them.

"We'll be speaking off the record, Mrs. McNulty," the chancellor said to his secretary, "so we won't need a transcript."

"Very well, Your Grace." She, too, left.

"Now there is only us," the chancellor said to Maria and McKensie, "so I shall speak freely and invite you to do the same. Is that agreeable?"

"Yes, Your Grace," they responded.

The chancellor opened the manila folder and took out the copy of Karen Rolf's article that Maguire and Seamus had copied in the library. "Let's all try to be perfectly honest, so from out outset, I'll tell you that we have a good idea where Professor O'Donnell has gone." He tossed the article on the table. "Easy enough to check out." He looked at Maria. "Correct, miss?"

Maria remained silent.

The chancellor rose and went to a sideboard beneath the window. He fumbled with a key then opened a small door and took out a bottle of Scotch whiskey and glasses. He poured himself a drink, and said, "Please help yourselves." McKensie, grateful for the opportunity, obliged. Maria declined.

The chancellor settled back in his chair and sipped his Scotch. "I got this job," he said, "because I'm a good politician. I make no pretence at academics. I see to it that your salaries are competitive and that your work environment is roughly comparable to any in the U.K.. That's my job. Your job is to teach, research and publish and make sure that your scholarly output is comparable to any in the U.K.. Ordinarily, our jobs do not conflict, but occasionally they do."

The chancellor paused and sipped his Scotch, then continued. He looked directly at Maria.

"When they do, politics is inclined to take precedence. For example, in our physics, chemistry and biological laboratories, some research is classified under the Official Secrets Act. The researchers are not free to disseminate information as they choose. Even in your own field, Dr. Burke, psychological profiles of hijackers, terrorists, and such are still classified secret. No rational person would challenge the need for such secrecy."

The chancellor leaned closer, set his drink on the table, and lowered his voice.

"For the first time in my memory, Professor O'Donnell has presented us with information in the field of anthropology that impinges so importantly on world politics and the stability of governments, that politics must claim precedence over the usual academic processes."

"Perhaps the importance of Professor O'Donnell's work has been exaggerated," Maria said.

The chancellor sipped his drink thoughtfully. "The political experts don't think so," he said. "World politics are in crisis. The map of Europe is being redrawn, Africa is undergoing profound changes as is Central and South America. At this very dangerous time when new leadership is emerging all over the world, Professor O'Donnell chooses to inform us that a superior breed of human being has evolved on the planet. Well, not likely. World politics says, no, we do not want this information at this time.

"Such was the case regarding the findings of the Warren Commission on the assassination of President Kennedy, and the military secrets developed in our own laboratories, and the profiles developed by world psychologists. Perhaps in the future the timing will be better. At the moment, the academic process must yield to politics in this matter. Do you understand, Miss Burke?"

Maria hesitated. "Yes, but I'm not sure I agree."

"There isn't a Chief Executive Officer or politician in the world, including myself, who would tolerate being driven out of office because he (or she) may be an inferior kind of human." The chancellor reddened in the face. "In fact, there are agencies who would be tempted to remove the messenger who bears such bad news. Do I make myself clear, Miss Burke?"

"And what about truth and academic freedom," Maria asked, "and censorship? Politicians have a history of suppressing unpopular ideas that disturb the status quo. How does one distinguish between what is genuinely in the public interest from raw political expediency?"

"Sir," the Chancellor turned to McKensie, "how do you determine which research is in the public interest and which is in the self-serving interest of the individual faculty member? You do promote, don't you, on the basis of individual productivity?"

"We have a promotions committee, your Lordship."

"And how does the promotions committee distinguish between public service and self-service?"

McKensie sipped his drink and thought. "We have no defensible way of separating the two," he admitted.

"Thank you, Mr. McKensie." The chancellor turned to Maria. "So you see, objectivity is a goal toward which we both strive and a commodity that neither of us has cornered. It is our opinion that Professor O'Donnell's report should be not published at this time. We're asking you as his friend and one who has significant influence over his actions to make a good faith effort to convince O'Donnell to return to Northern Ireland. You have my personal guarantee that his position at the University will be secure and that all charges against him will be dropped. For his part, he must guarantee that he will not seek publication at this time. Further, I shall guarantee him promotion to the next rank based on his excellent and original work. That, Miss Burke, is our best and only offer."

"It seems reasonable to me," Maria said, "but I can't speak for Kevin O'Donnell. What would you consider a 'good faith' effort on my part?"

"A letter detailing our offer and urging O'Donnell to consider the consequences if he refuses."

"And what are the consequences?"

The chancellor rose. "You and he could lose your positions at this university and the police will be persuaded to press criminal charges against both of you. I shall turn the entire matter over to the British government which will seek O'Donnell's extradition." He paused. "You may have a day or two to consider writing the letter, Miss Burke. This office will be waiting for an answer." The chancellor opened the door to the outer office. "Good day to the both of you."

18

"You talk funny," the gunman said, rubbing the muzzle of his pistol up and down Kevin's ribs. "Where're you from?"

"Northern Ireland," Kevin answered, "and if we both don't get out of this car in the next few second, we're going to be blown to bits."

"What do you mean?"

"That wasn't a regulator for a heart pacer you gave that man back there. It was a radio transmitter; I've seen them before. He's probably planted a bomb in this car…"

"You're crazy as hell! Why would he do that?"

"You saw the gun, didn't you? He's trying to kill me, and he's going to do it any minute now. There's a bomb in this car."

The gunman thought about it for a few second. "I don't know…I think you're crazy as hell."

"Well, I don't know who he is or what he wants but I'm not waiting for you to make up your bloody mind," Kevin said. "You can shoot if you want but I'm getting out right now."

"Okay, stop the car!" the gunman shouted.

Kevin pushed the brake pedal as hard as he could, swerving off the road and onto the grassy shoulder. His passenger fumbled with the door, pushed it open and jumped out. Then he turned and ran back toward town still clutching the attache case.

That's right, you bastard, run. Any minute now the car could go up. Kevin reached around to the rear seat and grasped his bodhran. Any minute!

He wrenched the door open and with the bodhran in his hands, Kevin ran as fast as he could into the open field alongside the road. An explosion blew a wave of searing heat behind him, flinging the car into the air, tearing it to pieces and scattering metal and glass in every direction. The car burst into scorching orange-blue flames. Kevin flung himself to the ground.

He lay still, breathing into the earth, thinking how close he came—not minutes, but seconds. Welcome to America. He had no money, no identification except the fake passport in his jacket pocket, just the clothes on his back, and him a stranger in a foreign land. Mother of God, what a predicament!

The field in which he lay had been newly plowed and the earth smelled good, and didn't the earth smell the same the world over? He was alive, and that was something, wasn't it, alive and watching the crackling flames scorch the darkness with whips of dancing light? And didn't he still have his bodhran?

Cars were stopping, a small crowd gathered on the road. Soon the police would arrive.

"You all right, boy?"

The soft deep voice startled Kevin. He hadn't seen the black man approach across the field behind him.

Kevin got to his feet. "Aye, sir, thank you, I'm all right."

"What happened?"

"Och, it's a long story. Someone tried to kill me."

"Where're you from?" Suspicious. "You running dope?"

"Och, no, nothing like that, at all. I'm from Northern Ireland, a teacher, and I'm trying to get to the

113

University of Florida at Gainesville." Kevin paused and wondered if he could trust this stranger. He had to trust him. "I can't let the police pick me up. My passport's a fake."

"Northern Ireland," the black man thought out loud. "Are you a terrorist?"

"No, just a teacher."

Puzzled, the black man asked, "Then why do you have a fake passport?"

"Och, that's another story. Will you help me?"

"Northern Ireland," the black man said again. "Whose side are you on?"

"I'm a Belfast Catholic."

The black man laughed softly, deep in his throat. "Then get your lily white ass moving before the sheriff comes looking for you. Follow me."

He took off at a trot through the soft, plowed earth, heading for a set of distant yellowish lights.

"You right behind me, boy?"

"Aye," Kevin panted, clutching his bodhran and trying to keep pace with the heavy figure that seemed to float across the darkening field.

The house was small, a one-story cement block dwelling with an ageing pickup truck in the driveway. The black man burst through the door calling back to Kevin, "Hurry up, man, and close the door behind you."

Two young girls in their middle teens sat on the floor watching a noisy television show. Kevin stopped and watched.

"Good evening, young ladies," he said. "God bless all here." The two girls turned and looked at Kevin, and then at their father. "Who's he?" they asked.

"What's your name, boy?" the black man asked.

"Kevin O'Donnell from Northern Ireland."

"Children," the black man said, "Mr. O'Donnell's a teacher, and he's going to stay with us tonight." He held out his hand to Kevin. "I'm Orville Johnson, and these are my girls, Evangeline and Bitsy. You can't miss Bitsy 'cause she's the itsy-bitsy one."

"Papa!"

"And this young lady—" a tall, slender black woman had emerged from the kitchen—" is my wife, Natalie."

Natalie held out her hand to Kevin who marveled at the smooth, silky texture of the skin.

"Mr. O'Donnell's car just blew up on the road. You can see it from the window," Orville said. "If the deputy or anyone comes poking around asking about it, we know nothing about any car or anybody. Understand?"

The smiles began to fade from the faces of the women. Natalie looked at Orville with apprehension.

"No, nothing like that," Orville reassured them. "Look at him—who else but an Irishman would save an old drum from a burning car? He's a good man."

That was good enough for the family.

Kevin grinned and held up his bodhran. "My mother bought it for me. It's years and years old."

"But can you play it?" Orville asked.

"Och, a wee bit."

"That means he can play," Orville said. "First we'll have dinner—you hungry?—and then the Irishman will play for his supper. Fair enough?"

"Fair enough," Kevin said as someone pulled up a chair for him to watch television.

Heavy knocking at the door. Orville put his finger to his lips and pointed to the bedroom. Natalie pushed Kevin into the bedroom and closed the door. Again heavy knocking at the front door. Orville nodded toward the TV set and said, "Turn that down a bit." He opened the door.

"Good evening, Orville, sorry to disturb your dinner," the deputy said. "Have you seen anyone, a stranger, maybe, hanging around here? There's a car caught fire on the road over there and we're looking for the driver."

"We saw the fire, deputy, we thought it might be a gasoline truck so we stayed away."

"Well, it's mighty strange," the deputy said. "There's another fellow dead in the road up near the convenience store. The clerk says he's the one who shot her in the arm and robbed the store a short time ago. He took a hostage, some guy who stopped for gas, and they drove off in the hostage's car. We think that's the car that blew up but we can't find the hostage. The fire's so hot it melted the chassis. For all we know, the guy could still be in it."

"Who killed the other fella, the one who robbed the store?" Orville asked.

"Don't know. Looks like someone might have jumped him from the side of the road. Shot him dead, through the head."

"Maybe it was the fella he took hostage."

"Maybe. Anyway, keep your eyes open," the deputy warned, "and keep your women inside for the rest of the night. We could have a maniac at large."

"Thanks, deputy, I'll do that."

The deputy drove off. Orville closed the door and Kevin came out of the bedroom. "You heard that?" Orville asked Kevin. "You didn't shoot that man up at the grocery store, did you?"

"No," Kevin answered, "how could I? Haven't I been with you since I got out of the car? But I think I know who did."

Orville looked hard at Kevin. "My family comes first, boy," he said. "Are they in any danger?"

"No, sir," Kevin answered, "but I'll leave if you want."

"And where're you going to go?"

"I don't know."

"You have any money?"

"No," Kevin answered. "The fellow that robbed the store-the one who was shot—took everything, my money, clothes…"

"All you got is that damn drum?"

Kevin laughed. "Aye."

"That's okay if your momma gave it to you," Orville said, grinning. He turned to Natalie. "Feed us, woman, while I ponder what to do with this Irishman."

Natalie served fried chicken and corn-on-the-cob, and never in his life could Kevin remember a meal so delicious. The steam rising from the pot of corn on the gas stove, the aroma of sweet, frying chicken, the television babbling away in the next room, and the laughter and chatting around the kitchen table filled the small house with the smells and sounds of family. Kevin felt secure and comfortable. Orville poured a taste of red wine into water glasses and offered Kevin a toast: "Welcome to America," he said.

Kevin, squeezed in between Evangeline and Bitsy, struggled to his feet and raised his own glass:

> "I wish for you always-
> Walls for the wind
> And a roof for the rain
> And tea beside the fire.
> Laughter to cheer you
> And those you love near you
> And all that your heart might desire."

The girls clapped and Natalie said, "That was beautiful."

Orville said, "And after you play the drum for us, I'm going to take up a collection, enough to get you to Gainesville."

Kevin looked at all of them. "How can I thank you?"

"Play the Irish drum," everyone shouted.

A few miles south, in town, Joseph Hecht, clutching his attache case, pushed through the line outside the bus station. He purchased a ticket to Gainesville, Florida. He was in luck. A bus for Jacksonville was just boarding. Hecht shouldered people aside and climbed into the bus. His eyes were tired and red-rimmed and smoldered with silent rage.

He had to be sure. Goddamned Irishman. Did he burn up in the car or not? He couldn't take a chance. He had to go to Gainesville.

19

Although it was just past eight o'clock, the night was pitch black and the streets outside cold and deserted. A west wind gusted down the chimney swirling up sparks in the kitchen hearth. Maria sat with her brother, Phil, enjoying the comfort of a snug-warm house and the rosy glow of the coals.

"I'm in an awful stew, Phil," Maria said and told him of her meeting with the chancellor.

Phil listened, sipping his tea. When she finished, he said, "I know; I've heard."

"How could you possibly have heard?" she asked, just a little amazed at the speed news travels in a small town.

"Don't forget, I work with Seamus and Maguire."

"Those two!"

The floorboards squeaked in the upstairs bedroom and the soft buzz of conversation drifted downstairs, a reminder to Maria and Phil to keep their voices down.

"Well, what do you think, Phil," Maria asked, "shall I write Kevin and try to convince him to come home?" She re-filled the mugs with steaming tea. "Would you like a bite to eat? I'm going to have cereal."

"No thanks." Phil was silent for a moment. "I may be a bit over-protective," he said, "but I'm proud of you and your work at the university." Then he answered her original question with one of his own. "What do you want to do?"

"I don't know. I don't like the idea of the chancellor trying to blackmail me, but on the other hand, what he says makes sense. Kevin doesn't really have to publish immediately. He could wait a bit. That would satisfy everyone."

"Will he wait?"

"Probably not," she said.

"If delaying publication makes sense to everyone else, why doesn't it make sense to Kevin?"

"He believes he has made a significant discovery. He wants to publish and reap the rewards; it's perfectly normal. If he waits too long someone else could get credit."

"Exactly what is this so-called new knowledge that's causing all the trouble?"

When Maria told him, Phil whistled softly. "Whew! What if it's true?"

"Kevin thinks it's true and so must a lot of other people or he wouldn't be on the run. He needs supporting evidence and that's why America seemed like a great idea to me."

"Tell me, Maria," Phil got up and rinsed his mug at the sink, "is this man worth all the trouble he causes? We're talking serious problems here that could mean your jobs, your careers."

"Would I be going through all this if Kevin weren't worth it?" Maria replied. "And it's not just Kevin, although I'd do it all for him. It's the shabby, rotten way the university and the government went about trying to silence him. You know as well as I do that Kevin didn't have explosives in his apartment."

"Shh!" Phil said. "Keep your voice down. Let's not get Mam and Da all worked up; things are complicated enough. But you didn't answer my question: What do you want to do?"

Maria sighed. "I guess I'll write Kevin and ask him to come home. The university has made some concessions—"

Phil shook his head. "That's probably a waste of time, you know that. Once that man has made up his mind…" Phil shook his head. "Does his brother have any influence over him?"

"In this matter, probably less that I do," Maria answered.

"Who is Karen Rolf?" Phil asked.

"I don't know her," Maria answered. "I spoke to her on the phone and convinced her that Kevin could contribute to her project at the University of Florida. That's why she offered him a job. But if the police hadn't tried to arrest him on some trumped up charges, that wouldn't have been necessary."

"Well, let's be practical," Phil said, "what's done is done. The question is, can it be undone?"

"What do you mean?"

"Do you love this man, Maria?

"Aye, I do."

"Does he love you?"

"Aye, he says so."

"He certainly has a damn strange way of showing it. Do you think you could talk him into coming home and postponing publication before things really get out of hand?"

"I don't know," Maria answered.

"Is it worth a try?"

"What are you getting at, Phil?"

Phil went to the hall closet and returned with an envelope which he placed on the table in front of Maria.

"Here's a round trip ticket to Orlando, Florida," Phil said. "You can rent a car and drive to Gainesville. It's about a three hour drive."

"And what about my work?" Maria asked.

"You can have a week's leave of absence starting any time you wish."

Maria looked at the envelope. "Who paid for these?" she asked.

Phil laughed. "I knew you'd ask that. I did. Someone high up in the R.U.C. approached me with more or less the same deal the chancellor offered you. They wanted me to persuade you to go to Florida and talk to O'Donnell, try to convince him to come back to Northern Ireland and agree to postpone publication until they say it's okay. All charges against him would be dropped and he'd get a promotion—you know all the rest. They also offered to pay all your expenses." Phil paused. "I turned them down."

"Then where did these tickets come from?" Maria asked.

"I paid for them with my own hard earned cash," Phil answered.

"Why?"

"Because it's a good idea, Maria. You can go without any strings attached. You asked me what I think you should do? Okay, go over there and bring that hard-headed Ulsterman back with you before he wrecks his life and yours, too."

Maria sat silently for a few moments. The wind moaned down the chimney and sparks swirled in the grate.

"What date are the tickets for?" Maria asked.

"Day after tomorrow," Phil answered.

Maria reached out and picked up the envelope. She rested her hand on her brother's. "Thank you, Phil," she said, "you are the best brother a sister could have. Will you drive me to the airport?"

"Aye, but take care of yourself," Phil said. "I may sound provincial but America is a big place and you're on a dangerous errand."

20

The rumor spread through the British Airways Boeing 747 and even the captain of the aircraft, who usually paid little attention to such things, sent his first officer to investigate. The rumor was false, of course, but, reported the first officer, a passenger had boarded whose striking resemblance to Princess Diana was, in his words, "stunning". The captain, an unusually reserved man, made a mental note to check out this phenomenon sometime during the long flight to Florida.

Maria, who was used to creating these minor disturbances in Northern Ireland, was not prepared for the scope of the commotion she caused on British Airways. She did her best to hide in her book but attendants and passengers walked past her aisle seat again and again just to catch a glimpse of the beautiful young woman who so resembled "Princess Di".

A little girl about six or seven years old stopped in the aisle beside Maria's seat and asked her point blank, "Are you Princess Diana?"

Maria looked up from her reading, embarrassed. "No, I'm not," she said. "Sorry.

"Are you sure?" insisted the child.

Maria smiled at the little girl. "Quite," she said, "but I'm flattered you think so."

The plane prepared to taxi and Maria settled back and closed her eyes as the huge aircraft rumbled into place in the long line of planes waiting to depart. Maria had traveled to the continent many times, to France, Spain, Italy, and even to Russia, but this was her first trip to America. As the large aircraft slowly lifted through the mist and clouds, she couldn't help feeling a little apprehensive. She hadn't had time to phone Kevin. What would he say when she walked in on him?

The plane suddenly poked through the clouds into the sunshine. The huge cabin came alive with the buzz of conversation and the business of flight attendants.

At that moment, Kevin was also feeling a bit apprehensive. He had tried to smooth the wrinkles out of his clothing and comb his hair but the over-night ride in the bus, with it's delays and detours, had taken its toll on his appearance. He opened the door to Karen Rolf's office and presented himself to the secretary.

"I'm Kevin O'Donnell from Northern Ireland," he said, smoothing out a few wrinkles in his jacket. "Dr. Rolf is expecting me."

The secretary, the guardian of the departmental gates, looked Kevin over with a professional eye. This disheveled man with the funny drum under his arm could indeed be the expected Dr. O'Donnell. She said, "Just a minute, please," and walked back to Karen's office. Moments later Karen herself came hurrying out.

"Welcome, welcome," she greeted Kevin, smiling warmly and grasping his hand. "My gosh, what's happened to you? We were expecting you yesterday." She looked him over. "Come on back to my office and we'll…where's your luggage?"

"Ay, that's a bit of a story, Dr. Rolf."

"You mean it's gone?"

"Aye, that and a few other things. But I've managed to save the most important." He took out a rolled-up copy of his research project from an inside pocket of his jacket. "This," he said, "and this..." holding up his bodhran.

"Would you like a cup of coffee?" she asked.

"Aye, that would be nice."

Seated in Karen's office, Kevin told of his encounter with Hecht and of the attempt on his life. Karen listened, stomach churning, thinking all the time of Julian Zeiss and the strange manner in which he had been murdered.

"How strange," she whispered when Kevin had finished, "what's going on here?" She told him of Zeiss and his contact with Israel and the Mossad, and her suspicions concerning his death. "I think he was murdered," she said. "There's a connection—I know there is—between Dr. Zeiss' death and the Israelis, and since you're taking his place, you might be the next victim. But how on earth could they have found out about you, or am I completely paranoid?"

Kevin said, "I had to leave Northern Ireland because the government didn't want my research published. If I'm caught and extradited, I face a long prison term there so I don't think you're paranoid at all. If anyone's paranoid, it's Israel and Northern Ireland."

"Who is Dr. Burke, by the way?"

"My fiancé," Kevin replied. "She's a psychologist at the University of Northern Ireland. Did you tell her about your study?"

"Yes."

"Well, she knows all about both studies, so she may be in danger, too," Kevin said.

"Isn't it awful?" Karen said. "Why don't we forget about the whole business, it's just getting out of hand. I've hardly slept a wink since Zeiss was murdered. If anything happens to you, too, I'll never forgive myself."

"Not on your life," Kevin said, annoyed that she'd even consider abandoning the project. "Don't worry about me. I didn't risk my neck coming all the way from Northern Ireland just to give up. I'm ready to go to work, and the sooner the better."

"Do you have any money?" Karen asked.

"No, I'm sorry. Everything was stolen."

Karen made arrangements at a local bank for a line of credit for Kevin and requested her secretary to call finance and have them cut an advance check. "That will take a day or two," she said, "and you need money right now." Over his objections, she emptied her purse and came up with a little over three hundred dollars. "I can get more on the way home," she assured him. She had already made arrangements for a rented car which was parked in a slot outside the building. She handed him the keys. "Buy some clothes," she said, "and meet me back her in a few hours and we'll go home. I know you're tired and you'll want a shower."

"Can I heave the bodhran here?" Kevin asked.

"The what?"

"The bodhran-the drum—" holding it up.

"By all means," Karen replied. "I'm so angry and confused I may even give it a few whacks myself."

"Help yourself," Kevin said, "better than a therapist."

Joseph Hecht set his earphone down, stood up and stretched. How did the Irishman get out of the flaming car? The man had nine lives. He wiped the cobwebs off part of the small window behind the listening station in the bicycle shop and watched Kevin search for his rental car among the rows of cars in the parking lot across the street. It would be so easy; one shot from the pistol with the silencer…

"Don't even think of it," said the owner of the shop, as if reading Hecht's mind. He was a young man, unkempt, dressed in jeans and a dirty sweat shirt. He reached across with a greasy rag and smudged the area of window that Hecht had cleared.

Hecht moved aside.

"The company doesn't want you here," the owner said. "Your assignment was supposed to be completed on the road. This is only an emergency stop."

Hecht knew that, but circumstances had forced the change of plans.

"You've compromised your cover," the owner continued, "and that means you're known by sight. Take care of the situation or your worth to the company is zip. My best advice to you is to complete your assignment and disappear."

"Can I stay here for a few days?" Hecht asked.

"Last night was an emergency," the owner replied. "The company wants you out of here as soon as possible. If you compromise this operation, Mr. Hecht, you'll be as rare as one of your books."

This bicycle bastard knows all about me. That son-of-a-bitch Irishman!

"This is a scientific information gathering post," the owner said. "We have different assignments, and they conflict. Do you understand that, Mr. Hecht? You must e gone in a few days."

"I understand. Do you have a car?" Hecht asked.

"Take a bicycle."

Hecht had lost the one advantage that had guaranteed him success, death by surprise. Kevin would be expecting him. He would have to be creative.

He returned to the listening console and slipped the earphones over his head.

21

Small sparks like spilled diamonds scattered over the hearth then blinked out. Phil Burke leaned back in his old chair, stockinged feet jutting into the fireplace. He belched.

"Phil!" his mother said.

"Sorry, mam."

His father glanced at him. "Well, I hope you know what you've done, sending our Maria…"

Phil sighed. "Jesus, Da…"

"Don't swear in front of your mammy."

"Maria's a grown woman, Da, the trip will do her good even if she never sees O'Donnell. You don't understand. She had no choice."

"You'll turn your own kind against you, so you will, helping that…that…"

"Can I have a few minutes peace?" Phil said. "Bad enough I have to listen to this tripe all day at work without getting more of it when I come home."

"Would she be there yet?" his mother asked.

"Oh, aye."

"Has she enough money?"

"Yes, mam, more than she'll need."

"If he doesn't come back with her, will she get the sack?"

"Och, no," Phil answered, "she can't help what O'Donnell does."

"That—that—" his father muttered.

"Whsst! Enough of that," his mother said, "sure you're not helping anything with your carrying on."

Phil wiggled his toes and stretched. "Och, you're both upsetting yourselves for no reason at all. Maria is fine. Will you make a cup of tea before bed, mam?"

"Bad enough he's half her age, and forby, he's a papist," the father wouldn't let up.

"He's not half her age, Da," Phil said patiently, "he's a year or two younger, that's all. And if he's a Catholic, that's none of your business or mine. He does his job like the rest of us, and damn good, too, Maria says."

"Well, he'll never make much of himself, livin' in that wee huxter of a house…"

"It's an apartment, Da, and it's all he can afford on his salary."

"Will they get married, Phil?" the mother called from the kitchen.

"Och, I don't know, mam."

"I won't have popery in this house," the father said.

Phil shook his head in exasperation. "Believe me, this is the last house he'll come to, so don't worry about it."

The mother served sweet steaming tea in heavy mugs. They sipped and watched the coals sputter and glow in the hearth.

"We should change over to the gas," Phil tried to turn the conversation, "they say it's hotter and cleaner, too."

"Och, I like a coal fire," the mother said, "it's cozy and warm, so 'tis, don't you think so, John?"

The father grunted.

"I mind when I was a girl burning the peat," the mother said, "and nothing was warmer of a stormy night."

"What's this O'Donnell up to that has everyone in such swithers?" the father brought up the subject again.

"Och, it's just academic stuff, da, people like us wouldn't understand."

"If a bloody papist can understand, so can the cat."

Phil stood up and set his mug on the mantelpiece. "Well, I'm off to bed," he said. "I'd just as soon listen to the wind at the window than the wind blowing through here."

"Keep a civil tongue in your head," the father said.

"Would you carry a few wee coals up to our bedroom to take the chill off, Phil?" the mother asked.

"Aye, of course, mam."

Undressing for bed in their own room with the door closed and the small lamp on the dresser casting elongated shadows on the wall, the mother and father continued their whispered conversation.

"I want you to stop your bellyreggin'," the mother said, "and give Phil a chance to get his head shired when he comes home. I've never heard you take on this way before, John Burke."

"Och, it's not just me; you should hear what they're sayin' all over town."

"What?"

"That Phil helped O'Donnell out of the country, that he warned him the police wanted him for questioning. They say he's soft on the papists."

"We know our Phil better than any of them, and we know he wouldn't break the law."

The father stood in front of the few glowing coals in his long underwear. He rocked back and forth. "Not even for Maria?" he asked.

"Not even for Maria. Someone else got O'Donnell out of the country, and even the cat could work that one out."

"His brother?"

"Of course, so I don't want to hear you raring-up at Phil again. Now snib the door and come to bed."

The mother, a light sleeper, was first to hear the pounding on the front door. She woke, startled, trying to rouse herself fully. She shook her husband.

"John! John! Wake up, someone's at the door."

"Huh?"

"For God's sake, wake up! Someone's taking the door off its hinges."

Phil was already awake. She heard his creak past the bedroom door in his stockinged feet.

"Stay in bed," he called through the closed door, "I'll take care of it."

She heard the stairs creak under Phil's weight.

"John, get up." she shook her husband awake.

The front door opened and voices drifted upstairs, Phil's angry, almost shouting. In the dead of night. Cold.

Phil's voice raised again.

Two shots thundered through the quiet house. Silence. Then another shot.

The father, fully awake, crashed out of the bedroom and stumbled down the dark staircase.

Phil lay on his back, half in, half out of the doorway. At the top of the stairway the mother screamed. The father charged out of the door as a car dashed away, wheels spinning. The father chased it, in his bare feet, in his long underwear: "Bastards! Bastards! Bastards!" In the dead of night. Cold.

133

Out of breath, the father sank to the ground and looked back, knowing full well what he would see.

The mother wailing. A few lights beginning to wink on in front room windows.

Phil's stockinged feet protruding through the doorway.

22

Karen Rolf's perfume saturated the space between them and her eyes hypnotized Kevin. He barely heard a word she said.

"Kevin, for pete's sake," she exclaimed, "your mind's a thousand miles away." She snapped her fingers. "Anybody in there?"

"Oh, aye," he stumbled back to reality, "sorry, I was away with the fairies. Must be the perfume. It's distracting."

"Rubbish. Now talk shop with me for a minute. Some background data. The genus *Homo* may go back a few million years but dating is not our job. We should try to describe the conditions which may have led a particular species to diverge from the lineage. In other words, can we speculate about what triggers the evolutionary engine to start up, and why it kick in again about five thousand years ago? That's your job. I'm up to my armpits in mtDNA data." She paused. "Kevin, you're not even listening!"

The female graduate assistant at the other end of the lab grinned and squinted into her microscope.

"Oh, sorry," Kevin dragged his eyes away from those hypnotic pools of green, "Sorry, Karen."

Karen set her yellow pad and pen on a lab table. "Okay, why fight it," she said, "your jet lag is going to win." She smiled at Kevin. "Let's take the rest of the day off. No, wait a minute. A working picnic. Can you sail?"

"Sail what?"

"We can rent a sixteen-foot day sailer."

"Oh, aye, I can sail a wee bit. Where might one sail around here? I haven't seen any water."

"Big Bear Lake."

"Would that be B-E-A-R?"

"Ah, you're coming around fast, aren't you? Yes, Kevin, its' B-E-A-R, and while we're on the subject of four-letter words, we'll also do a little W-O-R-K while we're out there."

The graduate assistant giggled.

Karen instructed her assistant, "Martha, if anyone comes looking for us will you tell them we'll be in the field today? I'll double check with Kate, but I think my calendar's clear."

"Yes, Dr. Rolf."

"Maybe if we can thaw out this Irish flash with a little Florida sun he'll come to life."

The graduate assistant smiled and looked at Kevin.

"Martha, is it?" Kevin said. "Sure, that's a lovely name."

"Let's go, Kevin," Karen said. "I hope you sail a little bit better than you concentrate."

An hour later they were skimming over the water under a nice breeze. Karen stretched out on cushions in the bow while Kevin worked sails and rudder.

"I take it back," Karen said, eyes closed, "you're a wonderful sailor."

"Och, this is a bath tub, so it is," Kevin replied. "Come to the Antrim coast and I'll take you sailing in real water."

"No thanks, I hear it's cold there."

"Only in the summer months. The rest of the time it's unbearable."

"Brrr!" Karen shivered. "Too cold for a Florida girl."

Kevin found a little cove with a sandy beach sheltered from the wind and hidden from view. He eased the boat to shore and climbed out. Karen helped spread a blue plastic ground cloth and carry cushions and groceries ashore, ready-made sandwiches, cans of soft drinks, and dessert of cellophane-wrapped cakes.

Kevin flopped down in the sun, a sandwich in one hand, soft drink in the other. "What makes you think the evolutionary engine—your term, not mine—needs a trigger?" he suddenly asked. "Isn't evolution a dynamic, on-going process? We see it all around us. Species come and go every day. Right now, this very second, the life of something that was the last of its kind on earth may just have snuffed out—"

"And something new blinked on?"

"Aye. Isn't that the essence of genetics, change, instability over time? Catastrophe may modify, accelerate, retard, but the change goes on."

"'Over time', that's the operational phrase," Karen said. "In the past science had no way of tracking enormous amounts of data across time. No one noticed unless change took a quantum leap—"

"A catastrophe—"

"—and altered things within a time frame humans could manage. And since DNA was unknown then..."

"From the instant a species is born, it begins to die," Kevin hypothesized grandly, stretched out in the mid-day Florida sun, well-fed, soft drink in hand, eyes closed, feeling the warmth creep into his bones, "but the process is slow beyond human time comprehension."

"And every instant, somewhere, a potential species is under consideration at nature—"

"And thank god, nature in her wisdom, does away with most of them. Now I'm ready to take a nap," Kevin said, "so I'll thank you not to talk shop any more."

Minutes passed, or was it hours? Kevin was unsure. He only knew he had to find shade. The sun was unbearable. He sat up.

Karen lay stretched out on her back beside him, eyes closed, completely naked except for black bikini panties. Body lithe and tanned, breasts rising and falling almost imperceptibly with her measured breathing. Beautiful, beautiful, beautiful.

Kevin stared and suddenly he wanted her. More than anything in the world he wanted her, to touch, to kiss, to hold—

"Well, what do you think, O'Donnell?" Karen murmured without opening her eyes.

Kevin blushed; he thought she was asleep. "Och, I—I—you're—" He collected his wits. "Now wouldn't it be the sorry man indeed who couldn't appreciate that?"

"You can take your clothes off, too."

He thought about it. "I will not."

Karen opened her eyes and leaned over and kissed him, softly, quietly, brushing him with breasts and lips, filling his nostrils with the sweet scent of her.

"You're a witch, aren't you," he whispered, "come to steal my wits, my soul? You're a married woman and I have a girl in Ireland."

"Don't make life any more complicated than it is."

He touched her face and shoulders. "And I used to believe that Adam was such a damn fool, but that was before I met Eve."

"Take your clothes off."

"I'm going for a swim."

Kevin stood and unbuttoned his shirt. Get away, get away. He glanced through he branches of the overhanging mango tree. Two hundred meters offshore, creeping silently toward them in a small boat powered by an electric trolling motor, Hecht stood in the stern, one hand on the tiller, the other holding a gun, metallic, that glinted in the sunlight.

"Jesus, it's him," Kevin exclaimed. He reached down and pulled Karen to her feet. "Hurry! No time to explain. Grab your shoes, that's all, quickly. Hurry. Hurry."

Stunned, confused, Karen held back.

"It's him," Kevin urged, "the man who's been trying to kill me, and he's almost on top of us."

She grabbed her shoes and purse and, dressed only in panties, fled through the scrub with Kevin following. They stumbled through the woods for about ten minutes before they stopped to put on their shoes. Kevin pulled off his shirt.

"Here, put this on; you're scratched and bruised," Kevin said, glancing around, frantic, trying to catch a glimpse of Hecht.

"Do you see him?" Karen asked.

"No. Quick. Let's go. I hope this woods comes out at the parking lot."

"I think so."

They ran through the scrub, expecting any moment to hear the whine of a bullet through the branches.

Kevin knew that Hecht would be confused by the empty cove, but not for long. He would soon realize they had fled into the scrub and would quickly guess they had escaped in the direction of the parking lot. He would make every effort to overtake them in the woods. Perfect. No witnesses. He could set the boat adrift, create doubt. A drowning? A perfect setup, all he had to do was find them.

"Hurry, faster, you have to run faster," Kevin urged. "He's just behind us."

"I can't."

Then the shot came, just to the left, kicking up leaves and dirt. Hecht was moving too fast, he would overtake them.

Kevin looked around, grabbed Karen by the hand and pulled her down hard behind a stand of palmetto scrub. They pressed themselves against the ground, hoping, praying Hecht would pass to their front. If he came up behind them...

"Don't breathe," Kevin whispered.

Minutes later, wheezing, puffing, but driving straight ahead with the gun in his head, Hecht passed not twenty meters in front of them.

Kevin waited till Hecht was out of sight then he and Karen turned and ran back to the picnic cove.

"Let's use his boat, it's faster," Kevin said.

The key to the ignition was missing and Kevin didn't know how to start the trolling motor.

"Get out, get out. Into our own boat."

Karen climbed aboard and Kevin pushed off, towing Hecht's boat behind. He hoisted the sail and the wind caught it. They labored out from shore, slowed by the drag of the tow, but the wind was brisk and they glided steadily out to deep water.

They were about a hundred meters offshore when Hecht suddenly charged out of the shrubbery. He waded into the water as far as he dared then he raised the gun and aimed.

"Get down," Kevin shouted.

A bullet ripped through the nylon sail. Then another. And another. Then they were out of effective range.

"Is that the man?" Karen asked, pale, shaken.

"Aye, that's the one who tried to kill me, the one who probably killed your friend."

Karen made up her mind. "We're going to the police," she said. "This can't go on."

"Don't you understand, they'll deport me and I'll spend years in prison, if that bastard doesn't kill me first? I came over here to get away from the police."

"Well, don't think for a damn minute I'm going to sit around waiting for him to kill me," Karen said. "I don't understand it at all. Is what we're doing so damn important that people are ready to murder us? I don't think so. I quit."

"Did you recognize him?" Kevin asked. "He said he knew you and that his name is Levy, he's a librarian at your university."

"I don't know him, I never saw him in my life before and I never want to see him again."

About half way across the lake Kevin cut Hecht's boat loose and set it adrift. "What will we do," he asked, "we're both half naked, what will people say?"

"Around here? Don't even think about it."

"No, I mean at home, at your house."

"It's too early for David to be home," Karen said. "He wouldn't believe us anyway, and if he did, he'd just call the police. It's better to say nothing, I guess. But we can't go on running from this man, there's no place to hide."

"Do you have the keys to your car?" Kevin asked.

"Of course. I may leave my clothes but never my purse. Just like you and that damn drum."

"Bodhran."

They docked quickly, tied up the boat, and waved to the attendant. Barely noticed by the few people around the boat house, they climbed into Karen's car and crunched out of the parking lot.

"Where do you think he is?" Karen whispered, frightened.

"Whoever he is, the bastard's right behind us, running through the woods."

"God, that's scary."

"Will he try again?"

"Of course," Kevin replied, "unless I find him first."

"And do what?"

"Would you rather wait and have him jump us when we least expect it?" Kevin asked.

"No, I'd rather put an end to this nonsense and go to the police."

"I've told you, I can't go to the police."

David's car was in the driveway when they drove up. "Damn!" Karen said. "Okay, let me handle this, be cool."

"Be cool? And you with my shirt on and little else?"

"Shut up, Kevin. Leave David to me. Just go to your room."

Karen creaked open the front door and they crept into the foyer.

"Kevin!"

Kevin turned at the sound of the familiar voice. David and Maria stood waiting for them in the living room.

23

The owner of the bicycle shop tossed the evening newspaper across the counter to Hecht. "Take a look on page 14 and tell me if that guy looks familiar," he said.

Hecht quickly thumbed through the paper and found an artist's sketch of himself. The accompanying story reported that the county sheriff's department had been notified by the owners of Big Bear Lake boat rentals that one of their customers had failed to check in and the boat he had rented had been found adrift. The sheriff's department had no reason to suspect foul play but did not rule out accidental drowning. The area around the lake would be searched as soon as possible. Meanwhile, anyone with information about the person in the sketch should contact the sheriff's office.

"You're losing your touch," the owner said. "Was this connected with your assignment?"

Hecht mumbled something.

"What did you say?" the owner asked.

"I said, yes, I thought I had the both of them cold. Bad luck, that's all."

"Both of them? Your orders are to terminate the Irishman. If you harm the woman you could start an investigation."

"She was with him."

"The owner looked at Hecht and said nothing for a few seconds. Then he continued. "You know you can't change orders. I shouldn't have to tell you your business."

144

Hecht sighed. "It's the Irishman."

The owner nodded. "Right. I think you've something personal going on with this guy. The company does, too."

A loud alarm blasted in Hecht's head.

"What the hell do you mean, 'the company does, too?'" he demanded.

"I called them when I saw the paper, that's my job, you know that."

Hecht tried to mask the anger that swept through him. "You son-of-a-bitch," he whispered, "you and your two-bit bicycle..."

"Hey, hey," the owner tried to appease him, "take it easy, man. You know this business has its twists and turns. The company says there's no sense in wasting a good man on this job any longer. Too dangerous. Your cover's blown; your face is all over the paper. You fucked up; what you did today was stupid. Agreed?"

Hecht said nothing, he just glared at the owner.

"Okay. That's that. You have to get out of here. Pronto. But before you do, the company has ordered the both of us to get the paperwork you signed at the boat rental place. You did sign a rental form, didn't you?"

"Yes," Hecht mumbled.

"Okay, the sheriff's department will be around there tomorrow looking for those forms, they'll check handwriting, fingerprints, who the hell knows what. Anyway, the company has ordered us to break in tonight and get anything with your signature or fingerprints on it."

"What the hell are you talking about? If they can't find those rental papers the whole thing will look even more suspicious," Hecht said.

The owner shook his head. "Man, you're not thinking. We know that. They can be suspicious till this ass falls out but if they don't have concrete evidence like fingerprints or handwriting all they have is that half-assed drawing in the paper. If we can get the rental forms we might be able to salvage your so-called career and the company can still use you. Otherwise…"

"Otherwise what?"

The owner looked into Hecht's eyes. "Otherwise your usefulness is ended and you'd better plan on early retirement to Israel."

Hecht remained silent.

"In this business you're not allowed one mistake," the owner said, "but the company thinks it's worth the risk to my operation to try and pull your fat out of the fire. I don't like putting my ass on the line for you, I'm not a burglar, but if the company says so, then I'll try my hand at burglary. Can you pick a lock?"

Hecht glared at the owner. "Can you pick your nose? Why do I need you? If you want those rental papers I can be in and out of there while you're still bitching about it. Give me your car and go take a hike till I get back."

"No way. I don't trust you and neither does the company. I'm in charge of this, understand? If you have doubts or questions, there's the phone."

Hecht glared at him.

"It's just after seven o'clock. Okay. We'll leave about two A.M.. I've already checked, and no one

146

stays out there overnight. With a little luck, we should be in and out in ten minutes. Did you happen to notice where they keep the receipts?"

"On the counter top. Mine will be in the stack, probably near the top."

"Okay." The owner shook his head. "What a screw-up. You're a schmuck, Hecht. When this is over, I'm going to drive you to Jacksonville airport and you catch the first plane to New York. Understood? Company orders. And I don't want to see you again, ever."

"Shut up."

"Now I'm going out to eat; you get to park your ass in the back room till I return. I'll bring you back a hamburger."

"I don't eat that crap."

"Good, eat a couple of tires." The owner got up and slammed out of the bicycle shop, locking the door behind him.

Hecht went over to the listening post in the back room and turned on the switch. Quiet. He squinted through the smudged window at Karen Rolf's office. Dark. He tinkered with the equipment and then glared at the building across the street. "You son-of-a-bitch," he muttered aloud.

When the owner returned about two hours later Hecht was stretched out on the cot. The evening paper lay scattered about on the floor and a small yellow bulb burned in one corner. The owner looked at Hecht in disgust, gathered up the paper and sat down in the corner under the lamp.

The hours dragged on.

About one A.M. the owner shook Hecht awake. "Let's go," he said, pulling on a dark sweater and gloves.

Hecht sat on the side of the cot trying to rouse himself.

"Come on," the owner urged, "we've work to do."

Hecht got up and began to collect his belongings. "I take it we won't be coming back here," he said.

"You won't. I've been here for seven years and I intend to stay."

"Where's you car?" Hecht asked.

"In the alley in back."

"Let me have the keys to the trunk to put my bags in."

The owner hesitated then handed over the keys. "Be quiet," he said, "and don't slam the lid. No one's supposed to be in the shop after dark. We don't want campus security all over our ass."

Hecht snatched the keys and left through the back door. When he returned in a few minutes he stood in the shadows with his back to the wall.

"Do you have a piece of cardboard and a pen, something to make a sign," Hecht asked.

The owner looked up. "Come on, Hecht, let's go." He saw the gun in Hecht's hand, the long black silencer screwed into the barrel. "What are you doing? Are you crazy, or what?"

"Are you going to make the sign or am I going to shoot you and make it myself?" Hecht asked.

The owner found the writing materials and sat at a small table with Hecht standing behind him. Hecht said, "Now print what I tell you in nice big legible letters: 'CLOSED INDEFINITELY BECAUSE OF DEATH IN THE FAMILY'."

The owner turned to say something but Hecht pushed the barrel of the gun against his temple. "Write," Hecht said.

When the sign was finished Hecht said, "Now sign it, nice clear signature."

The owner signed. He said, "I don't know what you're up to, Hecht, but the company is going to hear all about it."

"Ah, yes, the company, you rotten son-of-a-bitch. Do you and the company think I'm a moron or something?" Hecht's voice trembled with anger.

"If they thought you were a moron would they risk me and my operation..."

Hecht backed off a few feet and fired. The bullet passed through the fleshy part of the owner's forearm and buried itself in the heavy wooden table. The owner moaned and fell forward. Hecht threw him a soiled towel.

"That kind of talk is going to get you killed," Hecht warned.

"What do you want from me, for christsake,?" the owner said, watching the blood ooze through the towel.

Hecht stepped around the table. "I want straight answers or the next shot is between the eyes."

"What do you want?"

Hecht glanced at the bleeding arm. "You'd better talk quickly and then get to the emergency room. Tell them you were robbed."

"What do you want, Hecht?"

"Why is the baseball bat in the trunk of your car?"

"Are you some kind of nut? I play baseball."

"It's brand new. You bought it this evening; I saw the tag. Now I'll ask you just once more—" Hecht raised the gun—"and if you lie, you're dead. What were you going to do with the baseball bat?"

Quiet. Then…"It was the company's idea."

"You were going to take me out to the lake, whack me over the head, carry me out on the lake and dump me. That hick sheriff would call it accidental; I fell out of the boat and bumped my head. Why?"

Resigned. "Okay. Your cover's blown; you were endangering both operations, yours and mine. When the sheriff found you, the matter would be closed; just another accidental drowning."

Hecht nodded. "Ass holes, you and the company. That rental form crap was such insulting garbage, a child could see through it, all you wanted was to get me out to the lake and whack me. Right?"

Quiet.

"Right?" Hecht raised his voice.

"Right," the owner admitted, "and keep your damn voice down."

"Okay, I need a few more days here," Hecht said, "and I don't want you behind me with a baseball bat. Get into the closet."

"I'll bleed to death. Give me a break, Hecht. I've treated you okay. You know we got to follow company rules."

The owner opened the door to the broom closet, cradling his wounded arm. "I need a doctor, Hecht."

"Not any more," Hecht replied. He shot the owner twice in back of the head, pushed him into the closet, and slammed the door shut.

"Good night, sweet prince, you double-dealing prick," he said, "and don't start stinking for a few days till I finish up here."

Hecht peered through the glass front door. The street was deserted. He hung the sign on the door. Two or three days at most before someone came looking for them. Time enough. He stretched out on the cot and went back to sleep.

24

David Rolf hurled a pillow at his wife. "Double standard, my ass," he said. "When you deliberately embarrass me—"

"Oh, embarrassing me doesn't count"—she pushed the pillow aside with her hair brush—"even when I find that real estate bimbo in my house, in my bedroom?"

David sat at the foot of the bed watching his wife brush her hair. "It's getting out of hand, Karen, the whole damn thing."

"What is?"

"Whatever you're up to, for christsake. We have a terrorist living under our roof and a goddamn assassin gunning for the both of you. That's beyond fun and games, and you say you're not going to the police? Are you nuts? You have to go to the police. It's not a matter of screwing around with O'Donnell, although I wish you wouldn't. We're talking about attempted murder and maybe even the fact of murder if what you suspect about Dr. Zeiss is true."

Karen looked at David reflected in her dressing table mirror. "You wish I wouldn't play around with O'Donnell? Well, I wish you wouldn't set up housekeeping with every little high school cheerleader who wiggles her ass at you." She shook her head. "You have a nerve. For your information I haven't screwed with O'Donnell, but I've thought about it. Now get out of my bedroom."

"Forget the screwing," David said, "it's the danger, honey, don't you see you're in danger?"

Karen continued to brush her hair. "Why should you give a damn? I haven't seen you lift a finger to help, you're not here when I need you, you're off playing grab ass with…"

"Give it up," David raised his voice, "stop it." Then quietly. "This is not the time for that. I want to help. When someone tries to kill my wife, believe me, that focuses my attention."

"Really?" Karen said. "Someone has to try to kill me before I can get your attention?"

"All right, I can see this is not going to work. Okay, can you forget I'm your husband, can you do that? Can you talk to me like your attorney."

"I wouldn't hire you to—"

"Oh, god, You're an unreasonable woman. I give up." David rose and started to leave.

"Wait a minute," Karen said. She closed her eyes and lowered her head. "All right, I'm sorry," she said. "I have to talk to someone. Please sit down. I'm scared."

David started to approach her. "No, stay where you are and let me finish. You said you would talk to me like a lawyer. Okay, be my lawyer."

David sat down, his eyes searching his wife's troubled face. "Whatever helps," he said.

"I've told you what we're doing but I can't find anything in our work worth dying or killing for. Yet Zeiss was murdered, I know he was murdered."

"You don't know, you think."

"I know they tried to kill O'Donnell."

"Who tried?"

"I don't know, and neither does O'Donnell, but I know someone tried to kill us both today. I saw the man. He raised his gun and shot at us, real bullets, they put holes in the sail. O'Donnell thinks it may be our own government or his. That's why we can't go to the police. He thinks it's a conspiracy to stop our study by any means, even murder."

"O'Donnell's nuts."

"Goddamn you, David, there you go again. Then you tell me why all the shooting."

"You're right, you're right," he said, "I should withhold judgment. I know better than that."

"Are you going to let me finish?"

"I's sorry, Karen, it won't happen again. Please go on."

"Well, that's it. What shall I do? Where do I go? If I call the police O'Donnell will be deported—he's here illegally—and my work could be confiscated. Is this study really that important?"

David rose and stood behind her at the dressing table. "Honey, you know I'm about as scientific as a potted fern but even I can see some serious political implications in what you're doing."

"Like...?"

"You say you may have discovered a new sub-species of human. Well, I say who the hell needs another species of human? We don't even know what to do with the one we got. And this would be an advanced species, no less, so there's a piece of propaganda that could frost many a set of political balls. You could start a world-wide firestorm. Honey, you and O'Donnell can't go around blind like Mr. McGoo destabilizing politics, to say nothing of private and public institutions and professions. Your ideas are too radical. Forget this damn study, even if you're right, give it up. Think about it, Karen, we have too much to lose."

Karen looked down at her hands. "It could be the best research I've ever done, maybe a Noble Prize. And what about the search for truth and all that?"

"You've a hundred good studies in your head; I know. And who the hell needs truth? As a lawyer I can tell you if everyone started to tell the whole truth tomorrow morning we'd be at each other's throats by nightfall. Society's built on ritual deception and don't let anyone ever tell you different."

Karen looked up at David's eyes reflected in her dressing table mirror. "Let's go to bed," she said.

"Will you drop this research and send O'Donnell packing?"

"Will you be a faithful husband?"

David reached down and encircled his wife with his arms. "I have abused and neglected you," he said, "but the thought of harm coming to you scares me straight. Yes, I promise you I'll be a good and faithful husband."

"Forever?"

"Ever and ever."

She cupped his hands around her breasts and pressed them to her.

Kevin and Maria sat across from each other in Kevin's room, both still fully dressed. Maria broke the long silence. "You've hardly spoken a word to me since this afternoon. Are you in love with her, Kevin?"

"Of course not, Maria. Did you travel 3000 miles to ask me that?"

Maria chose her words carefully. "I didn't ask to come here, I didn't even want to come, and now I'm sorry I did. I'm only a messenger from the University and the police.

Kevin shifted uneasily. "What do they want?"

"You. Come back with me," she said.

"Or?"

"You'll be extradited and jailed, perhaps I will, too, for helping you, and we'll both probably lose our jobs at the University."

"Is that it?"

"Aye."

The minutes dragged by and the silence was awkward. Maria said, "Och, Kevin, what's wrong with you? Someone's trying to kill you, don't you understand? Kill, Kevin. Kill. Dead. Forever. My god, Kevin, what does it take…"

"I'm still here, amn't I?" Kevin said.

"Och, you're lucky, that's all, you could just as easily be dead. You know that. And now you're endangering Karen Rolf."

"As if you really cared what happened to her."

Maria looked at him. "How can you say that to me, Kevin? Yes, I'm angry at the both of you. I don't know what you were doing this afternoon, half naked; you embarrassed all of us; yes, I'm jealous and afraid. But I love you and I care what happens to you, to the both of you." She rose. "Now find me a place to spend the night and a taxi. I'm not staying here with you."

"It's too late, you can't get in anywhere."

"Then I'll sit in this chair…"

"Come to bed with me, Maria," Kevin said. "We'll divide it. You keep on your side and I'll stay on mine."

"Not now, Kevin. It's not the time. Are you going to return to Ireland with me?"

"No, Maria. Can't you see, working with Karen is the opportunity of a lifetime?"

Maria reached for the phone directory on the night stand. "Okay, Kevin, I suspected all along this trip wouldn't work." She found a taxi company and dialed the number. The cab would arrive shortly.

"I'll phone you tomorrow and let you know where to bring the rest of my luggage. Goodbye, Kevin, I'm going home." Maria said.

"Och, be reasonable, Maria, I love you…"

Maria tip-toed down the stairs and out the front door. She stood in the shadows of the shrubbery and cried.

Karen Rolf heard the front door open and close and watched the headlights of the taxi flash across the ceiling. She lay wide awake, cradled in her sleeping husband's arm, knowing how it felt to be rejected.

25

Seamus and Maguire, sweating in their heavy clothing, pushed through the crowd at Orlando Airport. Seamus lugged an antique wooden suitcase, heavy and bulky. Maguire carried an over-the-shoulder piece of soft luggage. Both dropped their bags at the Avis rental car booth.

The girl behind the counter prepared the forms. "Northern Ireland," she said, "is that the same as Ireland?"

Seamus opened his mouth to say something but Maguire laid a hand on his arm. "Aye," Maguire said, "one and the same."

Later Seamus asked him why he hadn't corrected her. "Because," answered Maguire, "who in bloody hell wants to spend all day explaining the difference to a Yank who couldn't care less anyway."

As they staggered about in the sweltering parking lot searching for their rented car, Seamus asked, "Bearing up?"

"Oh, aye, don't worry about me. It's you with that steamer trunk that might need some help."

"Do you think we could spend a wee while at Disney World?" Seamus shifted the heavy suitcase from one hand to the other.

Maguire, red-faced, perspiration dripping off the tip of his nose, looked straight ahead. "Disney World, is it?" He shook his head. "Here we are, hamstrung, tryin' to find our way in a strange country and you want to go to Disney World. Jeezus."

"Just askin', for christsake."

They found their car and started it running. "Can you believe it," Seamus said, "automatic wi' air conditioning. I wonder how it works?" A blast of cold air blew across their faces. "Och, that's lovely."

"Turn it down," Maguire said, "are you tryin' to freeze me?" He fingered a road map. "We take the Turnpike to Interstate Highway 75, you understand that?"

"You're the one with the map." Seamus drove off slowly.

"Get on the other side of the road," Maguire shouted. "Jeezus. You'll be after killing us both, so you will. They drive on the wrong side here."

"Och, away, she didn't tell us that," Seamus said.

Amid a jumble of road signs they found directions to the Florida Turnpike and managed to set out toward I-75. Seamus drove and Maguire sat on the passenger side nervously fingering the road map.

"Keep your eye peeled for a chippy," Seamus said, "I could do with a fish supper."

"You're in the wrong country for that, man," Maguire said, annoyed that Seamus had distracted him. "You'll have to make do with a pasty with peas and vinegar."

"Pasties, then."

"For god's sake, man, I'm having you on. There's none of that stuff in this country. We'll be lucky if we find a hamburger. Anyway, there's nothing on this road, so watch your driving."

"Bloody barbarians," said Seamus.

More by luck than Maguire's map reading skills, they exited the Turnpike and blundered onto I-75— going the wrong way. Blaring horns and frantic

159

gestures by southbound motorists soon got their attention.

"Jeezus, get on the other side," shouted Maguire, "you're on a one-way street."

Seamus grasped the problem and the solution. He swung across the grassy median without missing a beat, and, to the curses and horn-blowing of northbound traffic, bounced into the fast lane and continued northward.

"Jeezus!" Perspiration glowed on Maguire's face.

"Is that a sign up there?" Seamus asked.

"Aye." Maguire squinted. "It says, 'Gainesville 62 miles', if we ever reach there, what with your bloody driving."

Seamus slowed. "Want to lend a hand?"

"Keep on going."

"I'm starvin' to death…"

"Get your mind off food," Maguire said, "and worry about how we're going to break the news to her Royal Highness."

"Aye, that won't be easy," Seamus said, "they were close, those two."

"Some say Phil Burke had it coming," Maguire said, "flaunting the law and helping O'Donnell out of the country. He cost the two of us a pretty penny, didn't he? We could've had O'Donnell long before this."

"What'll we do if we see O'Donnell?"

"Nothing. Our job is to get Maria Burke back to Glenards, safe and sound. The chief things she might be in danger from them who shot her brother." Maguire paused for emphasis. "And if we screw this one up, we'll be after looking for a new line of work."

"Is that right," Seamus said, "we're just her bloody body guards? I wonder why he doesn't want O'Donnell?"

Maguire lowered his voice. "I heard the chief on the phone and by the sound of it he was talking with someone at the top. Would you believe it, the Israelis are after O'Donnell, too, only they want him dead? We're glad to oblige and stay out of their way."

"What's their problem?"

"Who cares as long as they do the job for us."

"Doesn't seem right, does it? He's a papist all right but he's one of us," Seamus said. "I wonder—"

"You don't get paid to wonder."

"Aye, still it's strange, Phil Burke's death and all."

"Not so strange when you consider the enemies Phil made helping O'Donnell," Maguire said. "What's strange to me is how we haven't a clue who did it."

"We know damn well it wasn't the I.R.A.," Seamus said. "They would've given him a medal."

"Aye, one of our own paramilitaries, do you think?"

Seamus shrugged. "Who else?"

"You'd think his da would've seen a face or a license, what with him chasing the car half way down the street," Maguire said.

"Aye, you would."

"Well, someone has to tell her." He glanced out of the side window. "I wish it wasn't me."

"It's you, all right," Seamus said. "I'm not good at things like that."

"Suppose she won't come back with us?"

"She has to, for the funeral. She won't miss that."

161

"Aye." Maguire changed the subject. "Why did you carry that bloody suitcase when you knew we'd be taking the next plane back?"

"I thought we might have a day at Disney World."

"Sometimes I—" Maguire began.

"Don't say a flamin' word," Seamus interrupted. "I'm the one that's carrying it, amn't I? When I ask you for help then you can start complaining."

Maguire nodded. "Aye." Pause. "There's a McDonald's ahead, two miles. Fancy a hamburger?"

"I'd rather have a fish supper."

Seamus eased the car into the off ramp and pulled into the drive-in lane of McDonald's. "What do you want?" he asked Maguire.

"I'll take a hamburger and a coke," Maguire said.

Seamus stopped the car and called out his order. "Two nice hamburgers and two Coca Colas, please" he said. He waited for a reply.

Maguire glanced out of Seamus' window. "You'll be waiting here till doomsday," he said. "You just gave the order to the trash bin."

Seamus realized his mistake. Embarrassed, he pulled out of line. "Well, then, kiss my flamin' arse. You can stuff your hamburger."

The car roared out of the restaurant, hurtled across the street and up the ramp to the Interstate. Amid the blaring of horns and a ballet of obscene gestures, Seamus forced his way into the traffic and continued the journey toward Gainesville.

Maguire was too terrified to laugh.

About an hour later Seamus said, "Gainesville next three exits. Which one?"

"Number two," Maguire said. "I've always fancied number two."

"Maybe it's because you have a lot in common, what."

"Aye, and you've lost your bap."

They exited the highway and pulled into the driveway of the nearest motel. Fifteen minutes and a half dozen quarters later, Maguire hung up the lobby phone and said, "She's staying at the Ramada Inn, wherever the hell that is."

Seamus pointed to the sign just outside the front door. It read, "Ramada Inn."

Room 118. Maguire took a deep breath and knocked.

The door opened, and Maria, eyes red-rimmed, gasped in surprise.

26

"Lady, lady in the land
Bear a tickle in your hand.
If you laugh or if you smile
You'll never be a lady's child."

Maria tried to keep from bursting into laughter but inevitably she did. Then Phil had his turn. He thrust out his hand and endured, unsmiling, while the tip of her finger gently explored his outstretched palm, searching for the magic place that sometimes broke through his composure. Phil at ten years old was already his own man.

Even when she had given up on learning to ride her two-wheel bicycle Phil came through for her. "You can ride it," he said. When Phil spoke like that, doubts vanished. She climbed on and he held her upright.

"Don't think about it," he said, "just pedal and feel the balance." Funny, she never thought of Phil as a child although he was only three years older. His voice was authority. He could command the wind and the sea. He could command her to ride the two-wheeler, and she did.

"Rain, rain, go to Spain,
Never show your face again."

They waded through puddles and leaped across ditches, and together in their yellow macs they splashed to school. Her protector. Her big brother. In

the late afternoons for an hour before the sun went
down, Phil suggested the games:

> "Some say the Divil's dead,
> Some say he's hardly,
> Some say the Divil's dead
> And buried in Killarney."

How could her Phil be dead?

> "Zed, zed, sugar on your bread…"

"Did you say something, miss?" Seamus asked.

"Och, no," she said, "just talking to myself." The
sun hung low, dazzling yellow, over Paines Prairie just
south of Gainesville.

"It's a couple of hour's drive," Seamus said, "but
we'll stop anywhere you wish. Are you hungry?"

"No, thank you," Maria answered, "I just want to
go home."

"Aye." Seamus angled into the fast lane. "We'll
be on the plane by half-past eight."

"Did you see Kevin O'Donnell when you picked
up my luggage?" Maria asked.

"No, miss," Maguire answered. "A gentleman
handed your bag to me out the front door. It wasn't
O'Donnell."

"Did you leave a message for Kevin?"

"Aye, miss. I said you'd been called back to
Northern Ireland owing to the sudden death of your
brother."

Childhood didn't last long in Glenards. Just time
to spend a few years in school, to play a wee game or

two, enjoy the odd holiday in Ballyshannon, maybe scribble a first poem on the pavement…

> Maria Burke is my name,
> Ireland is my Mother;
> Glenards is where I live
> And Phil Burke is my brother.

…and then childhood was over.

Once she caught the flu and Phil pampered and fussed over her till she got well. Naturally, Phil never caught it though he sat by her bedside day and night.

"Are you going to die?" he asked her.

The thought of dying never entered her head, she told him.

When Phil became a policeman it seemed the most natural thing in the world. Royal Ulster Constabulary. And didn't he look every bit the constable, tall, strong, full of good intentions.

> "Goodbye, Old Thing,
> "Cheerio, chin chin…"

Aloud, without thinking, Maria began to recite—

> "Up the airy mountain,
> Down the rushy glen…"

Maguire busied himself looking out of the window, embarrassed, but Seamus glanced over his shoulder and finished the verse—

"We daren't go ahunting
For Fear of little men."

They both laughed.

27

Kevin looked at the airline ticket that Karen pushed in front of him. "I'm not going," he said. He shoved it back across the desk.

"Don't be difficult, Kevin. You're off the payroll."

"Giving me the sack before I even begin?"

Karen reached across her desk and laid a hand on his arm. "No, dear, nothing like that. I just don't want people shooting at me any more. Enough problems, thank you."

"Och, you're exaggerating."

"Exaggerating or not, it's over as far as I'm concerned. My husband wants an end to it and so do I." Karen closed her folder. "I'm sorry to bring you all the way over here for nothing but it was a hasty decision. Dr. Burke was an excellent persuader. By the way, did she find a place to stay?"

"She's gone home, back to Northern Ireland."

"What?"

"Aye, she got word that she brother was killed. She left this afternoon."

"And you didn't go with her?"

"I intend to stay and finish," Kevin said.

"Not in my department. I can't believe you! You let Maria return without you? Why do you think she came here?"

Kevin reached over and took Karen's hand. "Maria wanted to know if I loved you," he said. "I told her no."

"Good." Karen tried to withdraw her hand but Kevin held on tightly.

"Come on, Kevin," Karen yanked her hand away, "let's be professional. I'm sorry if I gave you the wrong impression." She lowered her eyes. "I was angry with my husband." She patted his hand, "Now please, go home to Maria. Our project is ended as far as I'm concerned."

Then why did you bring me all the way over here if you haven't the guts to finish what you started?"

"Stop it, I'm not going to listen to that. Consider it a vacation, I'll pay you for your time."

Kevin rose and walked to the window. He glanced at the bicycle shop across the street and the impatient traffic honking through the intersection. "Well, then, Karen Rolf, it's been lovely but I'll say goodbye to you." He started toward the door.

"Where are you going?"

"I don't know, but I'll not stay where I'm not wanted."

Karen came from behind her desk and blocked his way. She put her arms around him and kissed him. "Don't leave like this," she said. "It would be easy to want you, Kevin, and I can understand why Maria puts up with you and your damn drum and your Irish eyes…"

"Och, you're playing with me."

She kissed him, lips parted and crushed him to her. He held her and stroked her hair.

"No, darling," she said, "you're playing with me but I'm onto your game."

"What game?" he said.

"Hah, the Kevin 'me first' game." She pulled away. "If you take me to dinner tonight, some place quiet and romantic, and then—" she kissed him "—

pack your things, and tomorrow, go far, far away—"
she kissed him again "—I'll still remember I have a
husband, and you have your own agenda."

She tucked the airline ticket into the inside pocket
of his jacket. "United to Boston, then Aer Lingus to
Cork. I assume you know how to cross the border."
She reached into the file basket on her desk and picked
up an envelope which she pressed into his hand. "And
six month's salary already converted to British
pounds."

"You've thought of everything," Kevin said.

"Not everything. How do I get my life back to
normal?"

"You think sacking me is the way to do it?"

She kissed him again. "I hope so."

The phone chirped in the bicycle shop and Hecht
snatched off the earphones, shuffled across the room
and picked the receiver off the wall.

"What do you want?"

"Hank, where's Hank?" a voice asked. They'd
called twice before.

"I told you, he went to Jacksonville for parts or
tools or something."

"Not back yet?"

"No, he told me if he finished late he'd stay over."
Even Hecht knew he sounded unconvincing but it was
the best he could do.

The caller said nothing for a moment and then,
"Well, okay, he's done that before." A damn lie. "Tell
him to call home as soon as he returns."

The phone went dead and Hecht knew his time was
up. A few hours maybe before the shooters came.

Quickly he scurried through the shop collecting his belongings and dumped them into the trunk of the car parked in the alley. As he passed the closet he noticed a trickle of blood seeping from beneath the door. "Hank, you stink," he said.

Before leaving through the back door Hecht returned to the listening station and clamped on the earphones one last time. He struck gold. He heard Karen say, "Okay, I've made reservations at Bruno's for seven-thirty." Great! One last chance to nail O'Donnell.

Hecht drove through the northeast section of Gainesville where Hank's car would not be recognized. He stopped at a sporting goods store and bought a Remington.30 caliber hunting rifle and a box of ammunition. He glanced carefully around. Israeli agents were smart and ruthless, but so was he, and he had an edge—he knew they were coming. He drove to Bruno's and surveyed the parking lot. Yes. Perfect.

Late in the afternoon he parked in a shopping center and planned his escape. He would drive to Jacksonville, abandon the car and take the bus to New Orleans. He knew New Orleans well, he'd find a job in a bookstore until he worked things out with the Israelis. Hecht knew his chances were slim, but perhaps he could convince someone high up that Hank was inept. Sooner or later Hank was bound to compromise the operation. Hadn't Hecht seen right through him? Surely he could convince someone in authority that he, Hecht, was too valuable to shoot and dump in a ditch, especially if he completed his assignment.

Okay. He gulped down a sandwich, dozed in the car and waited for darkness. Then he loaded the rifle, gassed up the car and drove to Bruno's.

Kevin stared, fascinated, as Karen leaned across the table, candlelight reflected in her eyes. Green? Yellow? Like a cat's, and I'm the bloody mouse. He shifted in his chair.

"That was a nice meal and you're great company," Karen said, "but what are you scheming now?"

"How to get you back to Ireland with me."

"Oh, oh, time for a reality check," Karen said. "Are you ready to travel tomorrow morning?"

"Oh, aye." He grinned. "Have I told you that you're the strangest person I've ever met, so you are? Suddenly I'm in America working, then just as suddenly I'm not. How many days has it been?"

"A lifetime."

"Och, things would get better."

"Worse," she said. "You're too dangerous for me, O'Donnell. You don't seem to understand; we were both nearly killed. You're naïve, or, as my husband puts it, you're nuts. Either way, you're out of my league."

"You're forgetting a man was killed before I even arrived here," Kevin said.

"I don't forget," Karen said. "That's why I'm dropping this project, and if you're smart, so will you." She laid her hand on top of his. "Will you stay in touch with me?"

"Och, no, what's the sense?"

"The sense is, I thought we were friends." She picked up her purse. "Will you drive me home now?"

"No." He tossed her the car keys. "Thanks for the loan of the car. I'll take a taxi back to your place tonight and a limo tomorrow. Now if you don't mind driving yourself, I'd like to stay on for a drink, one for the long road home."

Karen hesitated. "You're serious; you're not going to drive me home? That's not even good manners."

"No matter, let it all end here, now. Isn't that what you want?"

Karen stood. "Will I see you before you go?"

"If you're up early enough." He stood. "Goodbye, Karen, and thank you for a lovely time."

Karen took his hand, held it, then turned and walked away.

She climbed into the car and drove slowly through the parking lot. She turned left onto 113th Street.

Hecht waited in the shadows. He aimed the rifle carefully and squeezed the trigger. Crack!

Karen's car lurched off the road and crashed head-on into a pine tree.

28

The bouquet of wild flowers bought at the hospital gift shop seemed a pitiful token to offer someone who had almost died in his place. Kevin tossed the flowers into a trash bin at the elevator entrance then rode to the second floor.

"Is that you, O'Donnell?" Karen called. "I can smell your macho cologne a mile away." The top of her head from the eyes upward was bandaged but she sat erect in bed and Kevin could imagine those green eyes smoldering with anger in the darkness behind the bandage.

"Aye, I'm sorry…"

"That shot was meant for you," she said, "right through the temple. The only reason you're still alive is because I'm a few inches shorter. And god love the guy who invented air bags."

"I'm sorry…"

"Good-bye, O'Donnell, if you're still here when my husband returns he'll wring your neck. Go pick up your stuff in my lab and your luggage at the house, then catch your plane."

"You're all right, then?"

"Oh, sure, two black eyes, a detached retina, a bullet crease in my skull, a broken thumb, a few nicks and bruises—good-bye, O'Donnell, cheerio and all that, now out with you, and you'd better have eyes in back of your head because I'm sure that nut is still out there somewhere looking for you." Pause. "I might add, you deserve each other."

Kevin wanted to touch her, to reach out and thank her, but she would have none of it. She turned away from the sound of his voice. He reached over but she shook his hand away. "Please go, Kevin, now."

Kevin stood silently for a moment then turned and walked out of the room.

In the laboratory, his papers had been stuffed into a large manila envelope which Martha, the lab assistant, tossed into his hands without a word.

"May I use your phone to call a taxi?" Kevin asked.

"There's a public phone in the lobby, sir."

"Okay." Pause. "I'm sorry, Martha—"

"Goodbye, Dr. O'Donnell, have a nice flight."

On the way out of the Medical Center he stopped at the booth in the lobby and asked about transportation to Jacksonville.

"Sorry, sir, we don't have that information, try the Chamber of Commerce."

Even the taxi driver was rude. "Where you goin', buddy?"

Kevin entered the cab and sank into the rear seat. I'm a bloody jinx, everyone I touch ends up in trouble or worse. He gave the driver Karen's address. He'd pick up his few belongings and then...then, what? Did he have a choice? If he didn't return to Ireland, whoever was after him was bound to have another go. Sooner or later his luck would run out. He should have gone back with Maria; he would have, if he'd known about Phil. Poor Phil. Safer for everyone if he'd just go back to his cave; but then, he couldn't do that either, could he? That's why he was here in the first place...

"What'd you say, buddy?"

"Ah, nothing, nothing at all, just mumbling to myself," Kevin answered.

"Right, just what I need, a gentlemen right off the seventh floor."

Even before the taxi pulled into the driveway Kevin saw the clothes strewn over the lawn. The green and white boxer shorts, the white shirts, the slacks, the towels—everything he had bought a few days ago scattered across the grass. His bodhran, too.

The taxi stopped. "Hey, looks like someone dropped the laundry basket," the driver said.

Kevin looked about and said, "Will you wait for me till I get this lot together?"

"It's yours?" The driver laughed. "I'd say your old lady threw you out, buddy. Sorry, pal, I don't want to get mixed up in no family fight, pay me and I'm outta here."

The taxi drove away and Kevin picked up his bodhran. Nothing broken; even the beater was lying in the grass beside it. Good. He didn't care about the other stuff; still, he couldn't leave everything scattered over the lawn. He'd gather his clothes and dump them into the trash bin and then find a phone to get transportation to Jacksonville. He didn't dare use the house phone; he had no way inside, anyway.

He was bending over a stack of clothing when the car pulled into the driveway. Kevin glanced up, didn't recognize the car, and kept on scooping up clothing. Not until Hecht stood beside him with his gun discreetly covered and leveled at his chest did Kevin recognize him.

"Just drop all that shit and get into the car," Hecht said quietly, glancing around the neighborhood. "Get in the passenger side and slide over behind the wheel. If you even flick an eyelash I'll shoot you right here."

Kevin dropped the bundle of clothing and picked up the bodhran.

"Leave the drum," Hecht said. "you won't need it. You'll have a harp in a little while. And I'll take that envelope you're trying to hide."

"Stuff your head up your arse," Kevin said, "the bodhran stays with me, and if you want to rouse up the whole neighborhood, go ahead and shoot."

Hecht weighed the consequences. "That's okay, I have you, you son-of-a-bitch, drum or not, and you won't get away this time. Take the damn drum, when I shoot you I'm going to cram it down your stupid Irish face, you ass hole. You've caused me more trouble…"

He rammed the gun into Kevin's back and pushed him toward the car. "Throw the envelope onto the back seat and drive slowly and carefully, go where I tell you."

Kevin drove along University Avenue, stopping for lights and students in cross walks, searching for an opening, a chance to catch Hecht off guard, but Hecht had locked the doors, and the pressure of the gun in his side warned Kevin that Hecht was fully alert. A student on a bicycle dashed out from the curb, almost side-swiping them, and Kevin thought about brushing the bicycle with the car, creating an accident.

Hecht said, "If you're thinking what I think you're thinking, forget it, Irisher. I'll shoot you dead first and then shoot my way out of here. I've done it before."

Kevin believed him.

177

"Turn left," Hecht said.

A few minutes and three traffic lights later they were heading out of city limits. Kevin saw the road sign: "Waldo 8."

"We're off to the country, then?" Kevin said.

Hecht laughed, a dried up little scratching sound in the front of his mouth. "I'll say this about you, Irisher, you have two things going for you, nine lives and two brass balls," he said, "but it all runs out the first dirt road we see. The end of the line. Good-bye to you and your new species; you're about to have your nuts shot off by a member of the older genus."

"Who the bloody hell are you, anyway?" Kevin asked, twisting around to see Hecht's face.

Hecht pushed Kevin's face frontward with the gun barrel. "Keep your eyes on the road and turn onto the first dirt road you see. Now, who am I? Until you came along I was a pretty good Israeli agent."

"Israeli? What in hell do you want with me?"

"We want you dead; the U.K. wants you dead; the Yanks want you dead; the Arabs want you dead. In fact, we all want you six feet under. I had the bad fortune to draw the assignment to expedite your departure."

"You can't bury knowledge. Even James Joyce was finally published in Ireland."

"Screw Joyce and you, too. Who cares?" Hecht searched the road ahead. "In a few minutes you'll be able to bullshit with Joyce in person and you can ask him all about it." His eyes found what he was looking for. "There, that dirt road to your left up ahead."

As they drew closer, Kevin saw two or three rundown houses along the road. Who knows, maybe…

Hecht saw them, too. "Forget it," he ordered. "I said forget it, dim wit, don't you understand English? Speed up, don't turn here." He emphasized his words with jabs of the gun. "A deserted dirt road, deserted, understand? Drive on."

If Kevin could get his hands on the gun he could easily take care of Hecht, the wee skinny dried up leek of a man. But Hecht was unbelievably watchful, eyes darting from Kevin to the road ahead and back to Kevin. He didn't miss a trick.

"Do you know you almost killed Dr. Rolf?" Kevin said. "Can't you tell a woman from a man, big time Israeli agent? If the I.R.A. was after you, you'd be long dead, you pathetic amateur."

Hecht didn't reply. Instead, he raised the gun and put a bullet through the side window, just inches in front of Kevin's face.

Although the loud pop inside the car startled him, Kevin was expecting some sort of reaction from Hecht so he hardly flinched. The safety glass crinkled and splintered around the almost-perfect hole in the window.

"The next shot will be about four inches to the left," Hecht noted casually, "which should put it right through your big mouth. If you'd rather have it that way, I'll be glad to oblige, after all, you'll be dead in a few minutes anyway."

The menace in Hecht's voice was thick enough to clog the nostrils, so Kevin held his peace and drove in silence. Curiosity finally overcame his fear.

"One more thing," Kevin said, "how did you know where to find us—at the lake, the restaurant—?"

"You dumb bastards with your college degrees! The phone in Rolf's office has been tapped for days. Which reminds me. I'll take your plane tickets and your six month's salary—no, not now—I'll get them myself when I'm through with you." He ran the muzzle of the gun up and down Kevin's side. "Glad you reminded me, Irisher. Tell me, are they all as dumb as you in Ireland?"

"For your information, you slope-headed Neanderthal, I'm from Northern Ireland, a different country."

"Ah, that makes a lot of difference, doesn't it?" Hecht laughed like nails scratching across a blackboard.

Just ahead on the right, a deserted railway station, weather-beaten, grey rotting timbers, weeds growing through broken glass windows. "Ah, all sort of possibilities here," Hecht said, "slow down and turn right. Now I warn you, I'd like to keep this old car clean but I'll bow your brains out if you try anything funny."

Kevin turned right and eased the car down an overgrown set of ruts, once a gravel road.

"Drive around to the side of the building," Hecht ordered, "out of sight of the road. That's it. Park over there, and watch the broken glass, you moron, good, now turn off the engine and slide out after me. Keep your hands where I can see them."

Kevin climbed out of the car and stood with his hands by his sides watching Hecht circle around the car.

"Okay," Hecht said, examining the car's interior, "you're history, Irish. Nothing her to show you ever existed." He stopped. "Except that fucking drum. Reach in there and get it; take it out slowly and carefully, no funny business."

Kevin searched between the two front seats where he had set the bodhran. He grasped it by the rim and slowly withdrew his hand.

"Keep your hands where I can see them, Irish, I don't trust you, you sneaky son-of-a—"

Kevin backhanded the bodhran, like a frisbee, and the wooden rim thudded into the bridge of Hecht's nose and sliced upward into the eyes. Hecht stumbled backward and fired the gun. Kevin was on him in an instant twisting the gun out of his hand. Hecht managed to get off a second shot but it angled harmlessly upward. A moment later Hecht lay flat on his back on the ground, nose bleeding, both eyes swelling, while Kevin stood over him with the gun.

"I've seen a few James Bond movies," Kevin said, "and James Bond you're not."

Hecht spat anger from his eyes.

"I ought to kill you and leave you here, that's what you were going to do to me, wasn't it?" Kevin said. He looked around. "No one would find you for days." He looked down at Hecht. "You're a pathetic wee bugger, so you are. I think your nose is broken so you'd better have someone look at it." He picked up his bodhran. There was a bullet hole through the goatskin head and blood stains on the wood rim. "Ah, you shot my bodhran, so you did," and he shook his head.

"I'll kill you, Irisher, I swear to God I'll kill you," Hecht mumbled.

"Not today you won't," Kevin said. He removed the keys from the ignition and opened the car trunk. Inside he found a bicycle chain and lock; out of the corner of his eye he saw Hecht struggling to his feet.

"Good," Kevin said, "you saved me the trouble of carrying you. Walk inside the building, and don't fall through the floor."

Hecht stumbled up the decayed wooden steps to the door of the old railway station. He pushed the door open and entered a cobweb-strewn waiting room, deserted for decades. A dusty wooden bench stood alongside the wall.

"Over there," Kevin ordered, "sit down and empty your pockets."

Hecht dumped his wallet, spare change, and a plastic ballpoint pen on the bench beside him. Kevin glanced through the wallet. No identification, a compartment bulging with fifty-dollar bills.

"Wrap this bicycle chain around your waist," Kevin said, "and pass the ends back to me."

Kevin chained and locked Hecht to the seat.

"Even in your condition you should be able to free yourself in about an hour," Kevin said, "then if I were you I'd have that nose fixed." Kevin started to leave then turned back. "One more thing. I'm going back to Ireland so your job's finished. You managed to break up a good research team, you rotten wee…shit."

There wasn't any place to turn the car around so Kevin backed up the gravel path onto the roadway and drove back toward Gainesville. He stopped at a gas station for directions to Jacksonville. He had only about three hours to catch the flight to Boston; he barely made it as the last call for boarding rang over the loudspeaker as he rushed up to the check-in desk.

The flight to Boston was uneventful, leaving him time to collect his wits and catch a short nap. He fidgeted away the remaining afternoon waiting to board the evening flight to Ireland.

He finished a quick meal about six o'clock and finally gave in to a temptation that had plagued him all afternoon. He found the telephone number of Shands Hospital in Gainesville and asked for Karen's room. A man's voice answered the phone.

"Hello, David, this is Kevin. Is Karen able to reach the phone?"

Long silence. "Are you serious, you son-of-a-bitch? Do you think Karen wants to talk to you? If I had you here—"

Rattlings on the phone, voices, more rattlings, then Karen.

"Kevin? Where are you?"

"At Logan waiting for my plane."

"Are you all right? Did you have any trouble?"

"Och, no, not a bit."

"Kevin, I'm sorry for being so bitchy this morning. None of this was your fault. I'm sorry, dear, sorry for our project and sorry I never got to know you better, but I've promised everyone here that I'll drop the project. What about you?"

"I wanted only to tell you how deeply grieved I am for putting you in harm's way. You're a lovely woman and a first rate scientist." Kevin paused, not quite sure what to say next. "So good-bye, Karen Rolf. I still have the vision of you at the picnic locked away in a crinkle of my mind and that's the way I'll remember you." He paused. "Go raibh maith agat."

He hung up the phone and walked into the crowd.

The flight left on time, a Boeing 747 packed tight with a noisy crowd. The plane had reached cruising altitude when Kevin felt, sensed, something not quite right. Restless, he rose from his seat and squeezed past the other passengers. Perhaps a drink of water.

Three rows behind, nose bandaged, both eyes swollen, Hecht looked at Kevin out of bloodshot eyes as he passed. The eyes spoke.

29

Seamus held his breath as he watched the chopper drop vertically out of the rain-drenched sky onto the temporary landing pad.

"I didn't think they could do that," he said.

Maguire rubbed the heat-steamed window with an old towel to get a better view. "You don't think the Supremo wants to hang up there farting around waiting for a TOW missile?" He rubbed the corners of the window. "Down fast and into the 'six-wheeler' before anyone knows he's here. That's the way to do business."

"Why is he here? Seems to me there's enough trouble in Belfast to keep Intelligence busy. And why a civilian? I thought this was army territory."

"We'll know soon enough," Maguire answered.

The armored car roared across the soggy field, kicking up clumps of green-grassed clay. The Supremo sat beside the O.C., Glenards District, a paratroop colonel dressed in combat fatigues. British troops manned the gun slits of the vehicle, nervously rubbing the damp stocks of their FNs.

The weather was dismal, even for Northern Ireland. Sheets of cold rain lashed the air, whirling erratically in the gusting wind as if from a loose garden hose.

"Filthy weather," the Supremo muttered.

The colonel grunted.

The Chief Constable met the armored car outside the police station. He helped the Supremo, a man in his late fifties, down from the vehicle. "Hot tea waiting, sir; that should warm you up a bit."

"Filthy weather," the Supremo said.

"Aye, 'tis, that."

The Chief had cleared off his old desk at which the Supremo sat sipping tea, still bundled in his foul weather gear. The colonel sat beside him in a borrowed armchair. The Chief stood just inside the doorway of the tiny office.

"Close the door, Chief," the Supremo said. Satisfied that the office was secure, the Supremo said, "I want to do this quickly and be off. I'm here regarding the murder of one of your men, Constable Burke. Have you assigned anyone to the case yet?"

"Yes, sir," the Chief replied, "two men."

The Supremo looked around. "Bit crowded in here. Can we fit them in?"

Seamus and Maguire were summoned to the office and they stood uneasily beside their chief.

"Good," the Supremo said, "a word of warning. What is said here comes under Official Secrets and any person repeating any part of the conversation will be prosecuted. Understood? Good. Now let's speak freely about the execution of Constable Burke."

"Execution?" Seamus asked the question no one else would.

"Yes, cold blooded execution, in our opinion," the Supremo said. "From your report, Chief, we've concluded that Burke was executed not only by someone he knew, but probably by a member of a Protestant paramilitary organization."

"You've eliminated the IRA, then?" the Chief asked.

"Yes, they had nothing to gain by killing Burke. In fact, if your suspicions are correct, the IRA owed him a favor by helping Dr. O'Donnell out of the country. No, this was an inside job. Questions?"

Seamus shifted feet, the signal he was going to speak. "How do we know it wasn't just an attempted robbery or revenge killing by your ODS?"

"Sir," and the Supremo almost spat the words in Seamus' face, "I don't want to hear 'ODC' again. Understood? That's the sort of talk that's kept this country in a state of war and I won't tolerate any more of it." Seamus tried to fade into the wall. "There is no such thing as an ODC—an Ordinary Decent Criminal. Criminals are not decent, none of them—" he glared at the Chief—"and to make such a distinction between thugs and IRA terrorists is despicable. They're all thugs, the lot of them. I want this ODC rot stopped, Chief."

"Oh, aye, sir, you won't hear that again."

"Now, to answer your question. According to the parents' testimony, Constable Burke argued with his executioner for some time before he was shot. This indicates to us that he knew his assailant. Does that suggest something else to you?" The Supremo directed his question at Seamus.

"Hardly, sir," Seamus.

"Had there been open hostility in the community toward Constable Burke because of the O'Donnell incident?" The Supremo looked directly at Seamus.

"Ah, yes, sur, yes, indeed," Seamus replied.

"Gentlemen, if peace is to come to Northern Ireland the law must be enforced without prejudice." The Supremo slapped the desk with an open palm and the paratroop colonel looked at the ceiling. "Our Catholic neighbors are watching; so is the IRA.

They're waiting to see if we're as relentless in running one of our own to ground as we are them. I want Burke's murderer. Do you understand? If you can handle it, well and good. If not, expect my office to take over the investigation."

"What about O'Donnell, sir?" the Chief asked.

"Turn your O'Donnell files over to M15 and M16. Your task is to bring the Burke matter to a successful conclusion. Also, need I tell you we don't want further tragedy in that family. Questions?"

"Would you say a bit more about that, sir?" the Chief asked.

"Keep an eye on Maria Burke, she could be in danger, too, because of her connection with O'Donnell, also on the rest of the family till you make an arrest."

Then the Supremo was off in the roar of the 'six-wheeler' and the furious beating of the rain.

Seamus and Maguire watched the chopper disappear into the low overhanging rain clouds and the armored car splash north along the road to the coastal highway.

"What the hell was that all about?" Maguire said.

"When the civilian head of Intelligence for all of Northern Ireland leaves the comforts of Belfast for Glenards," Seamus said, "it tells me to get off my arse or my pension is in grave danger."

"You mean the Burke thing?"

"I mean we'd better find them that sent Phil Burke on the long journey."

Maguire rubbed his hands together. "That could be bloody dangerous," he said. "All it takes is a knock at the door at night."

"Don't open it, for christsake."

Maguire stared at Seamus. "Sometimes you talk like a fuckin' eejit." He shook his head. "And to think I depend on you to watch my back."

30

Kevin had about five minutes head start, no more. He rammed the little red Fiesta into gear and tore out of the rental parking. He knew the roads; Hecht didn't. He was used to driving these narrow country lanes on the "wrong" side, and Hecht wasn't. He had another advantage. Hecht would expect him to drive north, but instead, he headed south toward Kinsale. If only they hadn't given him a red car; he stuck out like a German tourist at the Giant's Causeway.

Hedgerows and foliage brushed against the side of the car as he streaked along the winding road, glancing frequently into the rearview mirror.

When he drove out of the airport Hecht was nowhere in sight, but the man was uncanny the way he anticipated Kevin's moves. How could Hecht miss a wee red car racing away form the airport?

Kevin glanced into the rearview mirror. Nothing; road empty as far as the curve behind him. But beyond the curve? Kevin's imagination ran wild. He pictured Hecht roaring down on him in a large black limousine, firing out of the window, ramming him from behind. The little Fiesta wouldn't stand a chance. A heap of metal folded like an accordion against a tree. Kevin pressed his foot against the accelerator and the car leaped into the air, almost careening out of control. Then—

Cows! Mother of god, cows, a herd of them crossing the road from one field to the pasture directly opposite, two busy little dogs snapping at their hooves, moving them grunting, complaining, splattering the ground, as they sloshed from one field to the other.

Oh, god, an interminable wait…fidgeting…glancing in the rearview mirror…expecting…engine revving, hurry, dear god, hurry…cows, wide-eyed, brushing against the car…young boy and elderly man waving thin wooden switches…shooing the animals through the gate. Hurry, dear god, hurry. Glancing in the mirror…

At the top of the hill a few hundred yards behind, a dark sedan, a Mercedes, roaring down on top of him. Hecht!

Kevin slowly let up the clutch and the car began to roll through the herd. Alarmed, the man and boy shouted, waved…plodding cows bumped to the side. Kevin pushed ahead.

The Mercedes roared into the herd and a cow went down, braying loudly, then scrambled to its feet and limped away, terrified. Barking and snarling, the dogs threw themselves at the machine that threatened their herd. The man and boy stood in front of the Mercedes, forcing it to stop. Hecht aimed a gun out of the side window and fired wildly. The herd stampeded. The boy ran around the car and grasped Hecht's gun hand from behind. The older man ran to help the boy and Hecht fired again. The bullet grazed the old man's cheek and he stumbled and fell. Hecht shook loose. Horn blowing, gun firing, cows knocked left and right, terrified braying and confusion, Hecht bullied through the herd and roared away. Behind, a scattered herd, anger and chaos.

Kevin drove for his life, glancing rearward when he dared to look up from the road. Less than half a mile separated them, but Hecht was reading his mind again. He could be driving into a trap. Nothing in front of him but the sea. Think, man, think. In the rearview mirror a dark sedan crested a hill.

Panic, then calm. Calm. If he didn't get a grip on himself, sooner or later this chase would kill him, a missed turn, a tree, a ditch, Hecht standing over his body, smiling. Out loud he said, "I've no choice. I have to kill him." Then furious, raging, he shouted, "You rotten animal of a man, you bastard! How do I get rid of you..."

How? Hecht gave him no time to think—the sedan almost filled the rearview mirror.

At this speed, Kevin reasoned, Hecht had to keep both hands on the wheel or risk losing control of the car. That's why he hadn't rammed Kevin from the rear. He was too close, right on his bumper, following every twist and turn as the road snaked southward. That gave Kevin an idea. Narrow as it was, this was the main road between Cork and Kinsale. Why not swing onto a narrower road where the larger car would be more at a disadvantage?

The Mercedes clung to him, dangerously close, too close for Kevin to do more than risk tapping the brake as the Ford rounded perilous curves. The slightest miscalculation and Hecht would ram the Fiesta. At this speed, that would mean disaster for Kevin. He concentrated on the road ahead, wondering what Hecht's game was. Hecht could have forced the Fiesta off the road into a tree, a ditch at any time. Maybe that wasn't Hecht's style. Hecht always had to be sure, certain of success. Here there was some risk to himself—definitely not Hecht's style. Ambush, execution, yes. From Kevin's own experience with the man, he reasoned that Hecht chose the killing ground carefully so as to minimize risk to himself, and this was not it.

Good. He slowed down slightly, gaining better control of the car. He hoped he was right. He looked in the mirror. The Mercedes had also slowed. For once he had guessed correctly.

Now what? Sooner or later he had to stop and Hecht would be right on top of him. The answer was to find a narrower road, a country lane where the smaller car would have a better chance of eluding the Mercedes. Or better yet, why not drive into Kinsale, right down to the dock? People were always strolling on the dock and witnesses would spoil Hecht's plans. That's it. Drive right into the heart of Kinsale, down to the dock, park the car, and lose Hecht among the narrow streets and shops. Kevin felt better; he had a plan, not much, but better than hurling along narrow roads hoping that Hecht would not run him into a ditch.

Hecht must have read Kevin's mind again because the Mercedes backed off, and Kevin could almost see Hecht relaxing, trying to anticipate Kevin's moves. Both cars drove at a reasonable speed and Hecht seemed content to leave things that way as long as Kevin didn't try to dash away. Kevin knew the little Fiesta was no match for the Mercedes, so whatever he planned, it must not include a car chase. He couldn't win and could easily lose his life.

About thirty minutes later both cars drove slowly into Kinsale which was surprisingly active for the time of year. In Kevin's mind, Kinsale was the New Orleans of Ireland (although he had never been to New Orleans), the musicians, the chalk artists, the strolling students, the relaxed and easy atmosphere. I could easily live here, he used to think, but no, Ulster was in his blood, his genes, and he had always returned to the storm-weary cliffs of Antrim, about as far away from Kinsale as Purgatory from heaven. The Mercedes broke into his musings, looming large in his rearview mirror, close enough for Kevin to see Hecht's pale pinched face assessing his every move. Filthy wee shit, I'm going to kill you.

They circled the town slowly, deliberately, and Hecht must have sensed that Kevin for looking for an escape route. *Port na Spaniagh.* A busy restaurant on Quay Street. Perfect. Kevin suddenly pulled into the only available parking slot. The Mercedes blocked him from behind, but out of nowhere appeared a *garda*, a policeman, who motioned Hecht to keep moving.

Hecht pulled forward a few yards and Kevin considered climbing out of his car and asking the *garda* for help. He changed his mind because Hecht would undoubtedly shoot him and the policeman and speed away. He needed a better idea.

While Hecht was still engaged with the *garda*, Kevin picked up his papers and bodhran, climbed out of his car and entered the restaurant. That would force Hecht to make a decision whether to follow Kevin into the restaurant (over the protests of the *garda*), or stand guard over Kevin's car. Hecht chose the restaurant.

Before Hecht entered the front door, Kevin had dashed through the restaurant, through a side door to the kitchen, and out a rear door while the kitchen personnel gaped in astonishment.

Across the street, down an alley, through a garden, across another street, an alley, across another street, out of breath, Kevin didn't pause till he was lost in a labyrinth of narrow streets and houses. He chose a house with a car parked outside, ran up the path and banged on the door. A young fellow about his own age opened the door.

"Hello," Kevin said breathlessly, "can I come in for a sec?"

"What do you want?" the man asked.

"Can't talk here; have to go inside," Kevin answered.

The young man moved aside, slowly. Suspiciously, "Come in."

"I want to borrow your car…" Kevin began.

"Fuck off!" the man exclaimed. "Get out."

"No wait, wait, hear me out. I'll pay you two hundred British pounds right now for the loan of your car for two days."

"Why?"

"Never mind that, will you do it?"

"Where are you going to take it?"

Kevin thought quickly. Where could he cross the border unnoticed in a crowd of day trippers? "Ah, Bundoran," he said, "I'll leave your car at Duffy's Car Park and tell them to expect you to pick it up. Do you know where Bundoran is?"

"Of course, 'way the hell up in Donegal. And how the hell do you expect me to get up there without a car?"

"For two hundred pounds you'll find a way, won't you?"

"How do I know you won't steal it, drive it across the border?" the man asked.

Kevin took out his passport and driver's license. "Here, copy the information. This is who I am."

"Are you I.R.A.?"

"No." Kevin opened his wallet and took out the pound notes. "What do you say?"

The man looked at the money. "Two days? You'll leave my car at Duffy's, in good shape?"

"Just the way you see it."

The man thought it over. "Three hundred pounds," he said.

You greedy worm. "Okay, three hundred pounds, that's it, take it or leave it."

"In advance."

"In advance," Kevin agreed.

"I'll take it," the man said, "but first I want to copy the information on your license and passport."

"Fair enough," Kevin said and handed over his documents. "One more thing—"

The man stopped. "What's that?" he asked suspiciously.

"Tell no one, I mean, no one about this deal, you never saw me, I was never here. You understand?"

"Hey, I don't want any trouble."

"No trouble at all. Here's the money, I'll take the car keys. What could be easier?"

The man watched Kevin drive away, secretly elated. The easiest three hundred pounds he'd ever made. He put on his jacket and walked down to the *Port na Spaniagh*. He told his friend, a waiter, who

196

agreed he'd made a good deal; for fifty pounds the waiter would drive him up to Bundoran tomorrow.

Hecht stood off to the side listening to the conversation.

31

"Oomph!"

The Delta flight hit, bounced, then fish-tailed down the runway, reverse thrusters roaring.

"Wouldn't hurt, a few hours on the simulator," the Israeli agent said.

"Crosswind," the American said.

"Third World country."

"Keep your voice down." The American glanced around. "Move your ass and let's beat the rush through customs."

"Shalom."

Bullshit.

"Ever been here before?" the Israeli asked.

"Once, years ago, but not to Cork. Shannon. Took the wife on one of those $1000 Killarney packages."

The plane taxied to the ramp. The American sprang from his aisle seat as the plane jerked to a stop, reached into the luggage rack, retrieved both overnight bags, dropped the Israeli's into his lap, and without further conversation lurched into the crowd.

The Israeli, tall, overweight and sweating in a dark rumpled suit, fidgeted in the aisle, trapped by hundreds of chattering tourists struggling to organize themselves and their carry-on baggage/

Forty minutes later both men assembled their hand guns in separate toilet stalls of the men's rest room. "Ready?" the American called.

The Israeli grunted. "Plastic crap." He had cross-threaded the barrel into the stock; now he struggled to unscrew it. He fumbled and muttered to himself.

The American waited.

"Okay." The Israeli banged out of the stall. "Where to? He can't be far ahead of us, two hours, would you say?"

The American checked under the door of each stall before speaking. "He'll be easy enough to find." He washed his hands and dried them with toilet paper which he crumpled and threw into a commode. "Let's get one thing straight before we start." He glanced around the empty rest room. "This is business."

"Business." The Israeli holstered his weapon and tried to smooth some of the wrinkles from his suit. "Looks like I slept in it."

"You did."

The girl behind the rental car booth recognized Hecht's photo. "Aye," she said, "I served him myself. We had nothing available but Mercedes. That's what he took."

"Did he say where he was going?" the Israeli asked.

"No, he didn't."

"Ah, too bad." The Israeli looked at the American. "I don't know what we're going to do. He was supposed to wait for us. He'll never find the house by himself, will he?"

The American shook his head. "I told him to wait."

The girl had an idea. "I'll phone the yard; maybe Paddy saw which way he went."

She dialed a number and spoke to the attendant. She listened, giggled a few times, said, "Ta.", and hung up. "South, he turned south, Paddy says."

"What's south?"

The girl shrugged her shoulders. "Bandon, Kinsale. Most Americans would be going to Kinsale."

The Israeli looked at the American and shook his head. "He'd have no reason to go south, would be?" He turned to the girl, "We need a car and we'll take anything you have."

"Sorry, we've nothing available right now. You might try Ryan's, next booth."

The Israeli started to say something, changed his mind, then mumbled, "Thank you."

"If your friend should ring—?" the girl called.

The Israeli hesitated. "Tell him we'll stay in—?"

"Cork," the American said.

"—in Cork for a few days. Get in touch with us."

They were in luck. Ryan's had a car for hire, a manual Austin Mini, barely able to accommodate the Israeli's bulk. After much wheezing and grunting he squeezed behind the wheel.

"Why would Hecht go to Kinsale?" the Israeli asked, backing out, looking over his shoulder.

"Following O'Donnell," the American said.

"Ah." The Israeli straightened the car, shifted into forward, and paced through the exit gate. He followed a truck to the highway and turned left. A direction arrow in English and Gaelic read "Kinsale".

They drove in silence for about ten minutes. The Israeli spoke first.

"How long have you been with the company?"

"Long," the American answered.

"Been to Israel?"

"Nope."

Another five minutes of complete silence. The Israeli said, "I was born in Dublin."

They crested a hill and ran into pandemonium. Flashing lights, police, ambulance, and struggling cattle in the road. A few spectators looked on. The Israeli pulled up next to a young boy with a cattle switch in his hand.

"What happened?" he asked.

"Some bastard ran into us. He got a gun, too."

"How long ago?"

"I don't know. Maybe an hour."

The *gardai* waved them through, "Carry on, carry on."

Hecht, they both agreed.

They rode another ten minutes in silence.

"I've been with the company eight years," the Israeli said, "mostly with Internal Security. I haven't done this kind of work before."

"Great," the American said, "he's not too far ahead of us."

The Israeli said, "They told me you're an expert. I know the country, north and south, that's how I drew the assignment." Pause. "What do we do about the other guy, O'Donnell?"

"Not our problem. He belongs to British M15 and M16."

Silence. Another few minutes.

"Hey, give me some advice, big shot," the Israeli said. "This Hecht's a dangerous man."

The American turned and looked at him, then turned back to the road. "Shoot first," he said.

32

The phone rang just as Maria entered her bedroom. She glanced at it, paused, then walked slowly to her desk and lifted the receiver.

"This is Maria Burke."

"Maria—"

The travel clock ticked on the mantelpiece above the fireplace.

"Where are you, Kevin?"

"In the Republic. If I give you a number will you ring me right back? No one has any change here."

Silence. "All right, go ahead."

Maria wrote the number on a memo pad and hung up the receiver. She removed her funeral coat and hat and stored them in the closet, sliding clothing along the rack to make room for the coat. She moved wearily, tiredly.

Now and then a recognizable phrase penetrated the wall separating her room from her parents'. Oh, god, was she up to another night of her mother's crying? Maybe now that the funeral was over...Kevin. Oh, god, she'd forgotten about Kevin. She dialed the number and Kevin was instantly on the line.

"Where are you?" she asked. "Are you coming home?"

"Aye. I'm in a pub. I haven't much time, Maria, can you help me out?"

"Of course, what is it?"

"Will you arrange a meeting with the chancellor, just you, me, and him?"

"Yes, I can do that, but what's up? Why do you sound so—so—harried?" Maria asked.

"Ah, I'm running, darling—or I should say I'm driving—for my life. That madman, you know, the one with the gun, has followed me here."

"To Ireland?"

"Aye, and he's already had a go at me." Kevin paused to catch his breath. "Listen, Maria—"

"Go to the police, Kevin, right now."

"I can't; they'll just turn me over to the Brits or the R.U.C. I have a better idea. Are you listening?"

Am I listening? Haven't I listed to you half my life, it seems? "I can hear you, Kevin, go ahead."

"I'll get across the border—"

"And how will you do that without being lifted?"

"Never mind that, I'll do it. I want to meet with the chancellor—"

"He'll expect some sort of compromise, Kevin."

"For god's sake please don't interrupt me, Maria, I don't know how long I have here. Aye, I'll compromise—"

Oh, will you now? After Phil is dead. After you've managed to wreck our lives…

"—but I want his protection. I'll talk to the Brits and the R.U.C. from his office only. Don't you see, Maria? If there's a shred of decency in the man—"

"There is."

"—he'll protect one of his own, especially if we agree on a way out of this situation. Then the Brits won't be dealing with just an individual. I'll have the university behind me. What do you think?"

Maria sat down in her desk chair and leaned back. What in god's name do you think we've been trying to tell you all along?

"Ah, you're talking sense at last," she said. "Aye, it's a good idea. The man's a politician but he's also the chancellor of the university. Give him a way to save face, appeal to his sense of responsibility for his faculty, make the project as much his as yours—"

"Why didn't you give me all this advice before—"

"Och, Kevin, who could tell you anything?"

"Aye, you're right, I wouldn't have listened. I'm sorry, Maria." Pause. "I love you."

"Hush, Kevin, we'll talk about that when you're safe. We'll make arrangements when you're across the border to talk with the chancellor immediately. He needs to know what you're willing to do, then he'll contact the authorities."

"You'll help me, then?"

"Haven't I always? But don't expect things to be the same between us, not for a while, anyway."

Silence. "What do you mean, Maria?"

"I mean I've changed, too. I've lost Phil, my brother, our friend…" Her voice whispered away. In the other room her mother wailed while the father spoke soft incomprehensible words.

"Maria, don't do this to me on the phone when I can't see you or touch you…"

"I'll make the arrangements you want. Ring me as soon as you're safe across the border. Be careful. The security forces are as dangerous as the man who's chasing you."

"Maria, do you love me?"

"I don't know, Kevin. We'll talk when I see you."

Pause.

"Ah, Jesus, god, the bastard's here, right outside the window! He's looking into my car."

"Who is? Kevin? Kevin!"

The contact was live but Kevin had vanished. Maria stayed on the line calling his name, but about five minutes later someone hung up the phone.

33

The borrowed car bucked and sputtered when he accelerated but Kevin managed to stay about a mile ahead of Hecht. Winding country roads, narrow and dangerous, prevented the larger car from overtaking. Kevin drove recklessly and he realized that somewhere, perhaps climbing the next hill or around the curve, the car would eventually give up. He could feel it in the engine vibration. The old car couldn't hole the pace.

Better do something while he still had power, but what? He searched the landscape ahead, watched the rearview mirror, thinking, thinking—

The ruins of a centuries-old abbey, jagged and black against a grey sky, materialized out of the green-brown hills just ahead. Kevin grappled with the alternatives and decided, spur of the moment, to make his stand among the ancient walls and overgrown tombstones of the abbey where he might have a chance to hide. The abbey also offered him a weapon, stones, stones against Hecht's gun, but not only stones, secluded places among the ruins, and he was younger and nimble enough to elude Hecht.

He swerved onto a grassy rutted path, bumped over rock-strewn ground and snapped off the ignition. He climbed out of the car and ran for the cover of a crumbling wall. A narrow slit marked the place where once a wooden gate had guarded the entrance to the abbey grounds. Kevin slipped through and ran across an open field to the roofless ruins. The west wind ruffled his hair and a few huge drops of rain plopped unnoticed on his head. Grey-black clouds hovered over the abbey ready to purge themselves of a pre-winter deluge.

Once inside the ancient chapel with its roof open to the darkening skies, nostrils full of the smell of moldering graves and damp earth, Kevin sought a passage to the upper level of an adjoining building whose barrel-shaped roof of stone was still intact and offered a high ground from which to see the road and approaches to the abbey.

The chapel, from grassy-carpeted chancel to nave, was a single over-grown graveyard which spilled over into the surrounding fields. Crypts and vaults and tombs of weathered stone decayed against walls no longer able to support them. Tombstones, centuries old, some fallen, others canted at odd angles, sank into the graves they once had marked, forming an obstacle course around which Kevin carefully stepped.

Skirting the sunken outlines of burial pits, Kevin searched the wall of the chancel for a stairway to the upper level of the adjoining ruin. He guessed that the second floor had been a dormitory with individual cells for the small congregation of monks. There must have been, still must be, a passageway from the chancel of the chapel to the dormitory above.

Muttering aloud, reaching out a hand now and then to steady his progress, probing for a break in the wall, Kevin didn't see the rusted iron gate buried in the grass. He tripped and fell flat, face down. And then without warning thunder growled in the sky and black clouds parted and a curtain of cold rain cascaded down and closed off the abbey from the living world.

Kevin lay quietly, winded, feeling the rain drench his body. Within arm's reach, buried among the rubble, he saw a wreath of red and white plastic with an opening in the center framing a brownish, weathered photograph of a young girl. How totally out of place. While the thunder rolled and rain lashed the weary ruin, Kevin reached for the wreath, then off to the side glimpsed what he had been searching for, a slight break in the wall, visible only from the ground, a stairway to an upper level.

He had torn the knees of his trousers and skinned the heel of his hand, but he forgot all as he rose and squeezed himself into the narrow slit between walls. A spiral stairway of stones, broken and tilted and sunken one upon the other, ascended toward a shaft of daylight about ten feet above him.

Those monks had to be tiny, wee people to squeeze up and down this stairway.

He emerged where once a wooden floor had supported rows of individual cells. Now, a narrow crumbling ledge of stone fringed a two-story drop straight down to graves and tombstones. Overhead, dampness seeped through the cracks between the stones of the barrel roof. A few narrow window openings spaced along the ledge focused the grey daylight spilling into the gloomy interior.

Kevin stood quietly listening to distant thunder, running his fingers over the snug fit of ancient mortarless stones, smelling the passing of centuries through this silent garden of the dead, and almost forgot why he was there till the roar of an approaching car jolted him back to the present.

Hecht had found him.

Kevin worked his way along the narrow ledge to the nearest window opening and peered out while clinging to a precarious hand hold in the decaying wall. Hecht had parked his car, and now, gun in hand, glancing around, he approached the abbey in the pouring rain, making no effort to shield himself from the downpour, splashing through puddles, oblivious to everything except—

"Me," Kevin muttered aloud, "that bastard really wants me."

Kevin scurried back along the ledge and searched for a stone large enough to do serious damage. He coaxed one from the wall, a large, blackish chunk of rock, jagged and sharp-edged. He wouldn't have been able to budge it except that the stone was already loose and ready to tumble onto the pile of rubble far below.

He struggled back to the window, carrying the stone under one arm while grasping for hand holds with the other. He dug his toes into the ledge and pressed his body so hard to the wall that he could smell the mold and damp.

He reached the window and risked a look. Hecht had vanished.

Silence.

"Hello, Irish."

The sound of Hecht's voice, high-pitched and excited, rising from the depths below, startled Kevin. There wasn't enough room on the ledge to turn around so he froze, framed in the window opening.

"There you are after all this time and all the trouble you caused me," Hecht said, "caught like a cockerroach on a wall."

Hecht laughed, dry, mirthless, full of rage held in check.

"No, don't try turning around," Hecht said, "I want to shoot you in the back, to make sure you're dead and leave you here among the rest of your kind. I don't know how you got up there but I know how you're coming down." Pause. "And what were you going to do with that big rock you're holding? You weren't going to drop that on my head were you?" Pause. "You stupid schmuck."

Time, Kevin needed time.

"Sure, you have me, don't you," Kevin said, "perched up here like a bloody parrot, and now what? Shoot me in the back? What a laugh you are, spouting great books and probably never read a damn one of them. Have you ever had an original idea in your life, Mr. Levy, or whatever your name is?"

"I have one now. First, I'll give you a little Robert Browning, and then a bullet in the head. How's that for an original idea?"

Hecht recited:

'We find great things are made of little things,
And little things go lessening till at last
Comes God behind them.'

"And I suppose you fancy yourself God?" Kevin said, measuring the distance to the outside ground which rose in a grassy mount at the foot of the wall. In the center of the mound was a puddle of water. If only there weren't hidden rocks.

"At the moment as far as you're concerned—" Hecht's voice grew softer—"yes, you might think of me as God."

And Kevin let the rock he was holding slip from his hand.

Hecht sprang back and fired, at the same time Kevin dove out of the window. He landed in the center of the puddle arms bent, and rolled the way he had done many times from the roof tops of the Falls Road flats.

A quick check, wet, muddy, and miserable, but nothing broken. He got up, soaking wet, and ran for the opening in the chapel wall. Already he could hear Hecht crashing through the rubble.

"Oh, you son-of-a-bitch," Hecht ranted, "you sly bastard, but I got you, you hear? I got you, Irish. There's no place to go. You screwed up, Irish, you should've kept on driving."

Maybe so, Kevin thought crouching behind a vault in the grassy nave of the old chapel, maybe so but we'll—

The muffled pop of a gun with a silencer showered him with stone chips.

"You stupid bastard I can see you," Hecht shouted.

No you can't, you're guessing. The old vault was built against the wall, so the only place to run was out in the open. If Hecht walked down the center of the nave and caught him crouching at the side of the vault, the game was over.

Another shot popped and a bullet ricocheted off stone and whined away into the pouring rain.

"All right, you son-of-a-bitch," Hecht said, closer now, "you're in here somewhere. I'm a patient man."

From the sound of his voice Hecht was doing exactly what Kevin hoped he wouldn't, walking down the center of the nave where he could command both sides. The rain beat furiously against the ground as streams of water rushed through time-worn channels.

Kevin crouched at the same of the vault feeling the strong currents wash the soil from underneath his feet. Glancing down, he shifted his position to gain a better footing in case he had to dash away. When he looked up, Hecht was standing over him with a gun.

"You look like a drowned rat," Hecht said. "Stand up and move into the open where I can get a clear shot at you."

Kevin moved toward the center of the nave, skirting the graves now awash in torrents of rain.

"I like that," Hecht said, following behind, "a man who won't walk on the dead. Good for you. Unfortunately, I don't share your scruples. Turn around, Irish, and get shot in the front, or run and get it in the back, the choice is yours."

Have I come this far to be shot to death in an old graveyard?___No way. Kevin turned and sprang.

Hecht stood behind a massive weathered tombstone, one hand on the old stone to steady himself, the other holding a gun leveled at Kevin's chest. Both feet were planted in the middle of a grave.

"Goodbye, pain-in-the-ass—" Hecht said.

In a twinkling, without warning, the ground opened up and swallowed Hecht.

Arms flailing, Kevin struggled to balance himself on the edge of the pit.

Then from the bottom of the grave came Hecht's voice, thin, shaking, "Son-of-a-bitch, son-of-a-bitch…"

Stunned by the suddenness of Hecht's disappearance, hearing Hecht's voice from the bottom of the pit, Kevin realized what had happened. Centuries of heavy rain on loosely packed earth had honeycombed the underlying soil. The present downpour plus Hecht's weight had collapsed the final load-bearing structure. The grave simply sank in on itself, not an unusual phenomenon in an ancient cemetery; the evidence was all around.

Hecht's hand grasping up from the pit jolted Kevin to action. He picked up a fist-sized rock, aimed, and threw. The rock smashed into Hecht's hand. The hand disappeared and two muffled shots exploded up into the rain-swept air.

"You son-of-a-bitch…"

"There's all kinds of rocks up here," Kevin said, "if you don't sit down and shut up, I'll drop a few of them on top of you." He glanced around and saw the red and white plastic wreath, and beside it, the old iron gate. If he could cover the opening of the grave with the grate…

Perhaps he could keep Hecht talking while he dragged the gate over to the grave. "That'll teach you to blaspheme the dead," Kevin said. "Are you all right?"

Then he crawled to the rusted gate and tugged and wrested it from its bed in the deep grass.

"What do you care?" Hecht answered from the bottom of the pit. "What th'hell do you care, mud, slime, god knows what…"

213

Kevin tore the gate loose and dragged it across the nave.

"…all kinds of crap. What are you doing? Are you going to drop something on me? I'll make a deal, Irish, you're a reasonable man. I'll toss up my gun if you let me climb out of here. You go your way and I swear…hey, what the hell is that you're going to drop on me, a goddam iron grate?" Panic in Hecht's voice. "Come on, Irish, you crazy son-of-a-bitch—"

The large gate crashed over the grave, completely covering the opening. Hecht fired his gun once more.

"You miserable…and what are you going to do, sit and guard me forever?"

"No," Kevin said, "I'm going to lay enough rocks on top of the gate so you can't move it from down there, then I'm going to drive out of here and let you rot."

Silence from the grave, then—

"Irish, no one comes here. This place is in the middle of goddam nowhere. I could be here for days, weeks; I could die from exposure."

"That's the idea," Kevin said.

Pause. "Okay, time for serious negotiating," Hecht said, "What do you want from me?"

"I want you dead," Kevin said, "you've been hounding me for no reason."

"What do you want, Irish, I know you're not going to drive off and leave me here to starve or die of pneumonia without giving me a chance."

Kevin hesitated. Hecht was right. He couldn't drive away and leave him buried alive in a deserted graveyard.

"Tell me what you want, Irish, and it's yours."

"The keys to your car."

The keys were flung up, hit the iron gate and bounced back, were flung up again and this time landed on the ground beside Kevin. He picked them up and put them in his pocket.

"Okay," Kevin said, "now the gun, pass it up to me, barrel down."

Hecht handed up his gun.

The rain fell in sheets, chilly and wind-blown. Kevin's hand and body shook with cold as he reached out and grasped Hecht's gun.

"Careful, Irish, don't shoot me by accident. Cold and miserable, isn't it? Why don't we just go home where it's nice and warm?" Hecht laughed, a genuine, normal laugh.

"I'll be in your car in a minute," Kevin replied, "with the heater on—"

"You better think about that. A Mercedes attracts attention, especially if you want to slip across the border; or suppose someone calls the hire company, and the company calls the police? People remember a Mercedes; remember all those damn cows?"

"Let me worry about that," Kevin said, "you just worry about keeping your own arse warm. I have one last question and if you put me on or tell me half truths I'll bury you in old tombstones. What's your real name?"

"I don't have a name."

"Answer me," Kevin said.

"My name is irrelevant."

"All right, I'm going to pile so many rocks on this gate you'll never get out."

"Wait a minute, Irish, wait a minute." Pause. "My name's Joseph Hecht; I'm an agent of the Mossad. Do you know who that is?"

"Israeli Intelligence."

"Hey, Irish, you'd better think of this: I may not be the only one after you," Hecht said, "what about the others? Wherever you go, someone will be waiting; think of it, Irish."

"All because of one damn piece of research?"

"Either you're the most naïve son-of-a-bitch I've ever met or the most dangerous," Hecht shouted above the noise of the rain.

"Go on," Kevin said.

"I was told you have evidence to prove the inequality of people, actual evolutionary data. Is that true?"

Kevin hesitated. "It might be."

"Then you'll never live to see the end of the year," Hecht shouted, "unless you say it's all a hoax and throw the crap away."

"Why, for god's sake?"

"You fool," Hecht shouted. "If God didn't create all men equal then democracy is a myth. And if the people in government aren't superior to the governed, totalitarianism will be challenged all over the globe. You're in deep shit, fella, unless someone get rid of you and your damn evidence. If they kill you they avoid the problem."

"For how long?"

"For now's good enough."

"And what was your job?"

"To kill you."

"You tried hard enough. Okay, I'm going to my car but I'll be back in a minute. Don't waste your time trying to get out of there."

Kevin sloshed through the rain and returned with a plastic rain coat. He said, "I can lay this rain coat on top of the gate and give you some shelter from the rain, or you can have it down there. What do you want?"

"Lay it across the gate. It'll keep the rain off me."

"Okay. I think you can work your way out of there in about two hours, maybe less."

"Maybe more. How about moving the gate from one corner, at least give me a start? The sides here are muddy and slippery and I don't know if I can move that gate by myself."

Kevin laughed. "I should bash you like the damn bug you are, or shoot you. You had every intention of shooting me."

Pause. "My job, Irish."

"Then be grateful for the break I'm giving you. I don't remember you ever giving me a chance any time."

"But you're a decent man; I'm not."

"Goodbye, Mr. Mossad," Kevin said, "I still have the gun and I may be decent but I'm not a complete bloody fool. If I see your hand reaching out of that pit before I leave, I'll shoot a hole through it."

Still, Kevin pulled back the gate and exposed an open corner of the grave. He also took Hecht's advice about the Mercedes; better to drive the old car and pass unnoticed. He let the air out of all four tires of the Mercedes. By the time Hecht freed himself, he would be across the border.

About a mile along the road Kevin flung the keys to the Mercedes out of the window. A mile or so further, after removing the bullets, he tossed the gun into a bramble thicket and scattered the ammunition. That should take care of Hecht for a while.

The Kinsale borrowed car vibrated and skipped now and then but if he held to a reasonable speed he would reach the border about twilight. Wet and cold but happy to be alive, Kevin turned on the heater.

Outside the rain slackened and the skies brightened in the distance. He would have preferred a thunderstorm when he slipped across the border. The British patrols would be less alert and it took more time to fire a weapon when it was carried barrel down out of the rain.

34

The chancellor reached into the sideboard for a bottle of Old Bushmills. "The brutal murder of your brother was a shock to all of us," he said, pouring himself a drink. "I know you and your family are devastated." He returned to the chair behind his desk. "But the good news is you convinced O'Donnell to return."

"I had little to do with it," Maria said. "That was Dr. O'Donnell's own decision."

"No matter, he's on his way. Now you said there were conditions..."

"Not conditions, Chancellor, just a few common sense precautions."

The chancellor sipped his whiskey. "Yes, of course, such as..."

"He needs your help with the Security Forces and the R.U.C.," Maria said. "If they pick him up before he reaches the University, he's convinced they'll ship him to an English prison. If they do, getting him out will be a long, drawn-out process, as you know."

The chancellor looked perplexed. "What do you propose I do?" he asked.

"Issue a statement to both organizations that the University encouraged Dr. O'Donnell's return, that you, the Chancellor, stand behind your faculty member, and that you will deal with the situation to everyone's satisfaction. Since you speak for the University, your statement will be taken quite seriously."

The chancellor raised his eyebrows. "Suddenly I speak for the University? O'Donnell didn't seem to pay much attention to me when he decided to embark on a self-granted leave of absence. I don't recall his talking it over with me or his department head."

"Dr. O'Donnell's a wee bit brash—"

"With no respect for authority." The chancellor sipped slowly.

"You promised if he would return—"

"Voluntarily. Even you must know he's not returning voluntarily. I've been getting reports that his life's been threatened—"

"Are you saying you don't intend to stand by your promises of full re-instatement, promotion—"

The chancellor sipped. "M15 wants him."

"M15?"

"Internal Security. I'm not sure if I can do much at this point. My interference would not be welcome."

Maria watched the chancellor toy with his glass, rubbing his index finger around the rim. "I understand your dilemma," she said. "You have to decide whether you're a politician or an academic. Which are you, really? I needn't tell you what this young university needs and expects."

The chancellor sipped. He glanced up and observed Maria carefully, remembering, for even his wife would not lecture him in this fashion. But then, how could Maria know he had grappled with that very question ever since he received her phone call? Indeed, was he a politician or an academic? Of course he was a politician; that's how he got the job. Why would he jeopardize his future by taking the wrong side in this issue?

"You are the University," Maria said, "as you go, we go."

"Well, I'm on the side of the law."

Maria looked, and her silence spoke.

"Was there anything else you wished to discuss?" the chancellor asked.

Maria stood.

The chancellor looked into his whiskey glass.

"Good day, sir," she said and walked toward the door.

Silence.

"Just a minute, miss." The chancellor cleared his throat.

Maria paused and turned.

The chancellor rose and set the whiskey glass on his desk. He cleared his throat again.

Maria smiled and walked toward him, hand extended. "Thank you, Chancellor," she said.

35

The rain had stopped but huge black clouds driven by a west wind tumbled across the sky; puddles of water brimmed over low depressions in the ground.

"What a miserable place," the Israeli agent grumbled, walking around the Mercedes, kicking a flat tire and waving the black plastic handgun which he used to point out the objects of his dissatisfaction. "Filthy ruins, mud paths, rotten roads, and now this. What do you think?"

The American examined the car. He walked around it, glanced inside, then opened the driver's door. Neat and clean, nothing out of place.

"Obviously, Hecht's still here or he wouldn't have left his car," the Israeli said.

"Or he wants us to think so," the American said.

Both of them gazed across the field to the rain-drab ruins of the abbey.

"He could easily ambush us in there," the American said. "I don't' see much protection, we'd be sitting ducks."

The Israeli gripped his gun and pointed it toward the abbey. "We could split up, one on each side. One of us might have a chance to get him if he shows."

"That's what he expects," the American said. "He's got a handgun, just like us, so he has to get close to use it." He paused. "Okay, first, let's get to the wall; when we're inside the grounds, you cover the back and sides, I'll take the front. We'll work as a team, shoot first, talk afterwards. Any better ideas?"

"You're the boss," the Israeli said, voice shaking, gun clenched tightly.

"Let's go."

They ran, crouching, to the wall, paused, then slipped through the opening. Ahead across the rain-soaked grass the abbey rose, dangerous and forbidding. The wind gusted in their faces, cold and damp, and smelled of musty earth.

They advanced across the open field, the Israeli walking backward, swinging his gun from side to side, the American watching for the slightest movement ahead. They paused briefly outside the crumbling chapel wall, then inched inside, guns drawn. Rain water dripped from old vaults and tombs.

"Cover me while I have a look around," the American said.

Gun in hand, stepping around graves, eyes roving constantly, he edged down one side of the chapel and up the other. He found the entrance to the adjoining ruin with the barrel roof and slipped through the narrow stone-edged opening. Dark and gloomy inside, illuminated by window slits in the wall high above; silent, empty.

Puzzled, the American re-entered the chapel. The Israeli stood with his back to a tomb, watching him.

Silence.

"Where th'hell is he?" the Israeli whispered, "There's nowhere to hide in here. This place gives me the creeps."

The American remained silent, searching with his eyes. He drew in his breath and said, "Is it possible he could have been in a ditch on the other side of the road? With four flat tires he doesn't have transportation. You didn't leave the keys in our car, did you?"

The Israeli slapped his pocket. "A fool I'm not."

"Maybe he took O'Donnell's car."

"I wonder if he knows the company sent two shooters after him?" the Israeli asked. "Maybe he expects us; maybe he knows."

"He knows," the American said, "that's why we have to get him; him or us, his mind works like that, and they tell me he's slick as a dick." The American thought out loud. "He can't be in here, we've looked everywhere, there's just no place to hide, and he could've put us down any time he wanted to."

"What do you want to do?"

"I'll go back to the car and check across the road," the American said. "If you hear shooting, come running. Take one last look around here and then come back to the car; we'll just keep on driving. Any better ideas?"

The Israeli hesitated. "I'd rather stay together and work as a team, like you said."

"We worked as a team; the place is clean, we've gone over every foot of it," the American said, "but in case we missed something, one of us should have another look around while the other checks across the road. We should've done that before we came in here. I can't be two places at the same time." He faced the Israeli. "One of us has to go over the area once more, foot by foot, and guard the other's back when he returns to the car. Take your pick. Which do you want to do?"

The Israeli didn't relish the idea of remaining in the ruin by himself but neither did he want the job of checking out the ditch behind the hedgerow across the road.

"Good enough," he said, "I'll stay and keep an eye open till you reach the car. Then I'll make a quick—"

"Not quick, you schmuck." The American was angry. "Slowly, methodically, go over this area again till you're satisfied it's clear and clean. If Hecht pops up from somewhere and shoots you in the back as you're leaving, or shoots me in the back when I'm walking to the car, I'll shoot you myself."

The Israeli watched the American cross the field to the parked cars, then he turned and began his final search. He and the American had gone over this place carefully and he didn't know where to start again. Perhaps among the graves in the middle ground. They had certainly examined the walls and adjacent vaults and tombs thoroughly.

He picked his way cautiously between graves, skirting rivulets of water rushing between them. He noticed the red and white plastic wreath and stooped to pick it up. Odd piece of crap. Still burying people here. Then he saw a rusted gate half covering an open grave, and a green plastic raincoat laid lengthwise across it, not quite covering the grave, revealing an opening into the pit.

He bent over and examined the raincoat without touching it. He and the American had searched for hiding places among the vaults close to the walls, looking into old tombs and the spaces between them. They wouldn't have noticed this raincoat hidden in the tall grass.

Of course, he could just walk away and leave it. Probably nothing, and peering into old graves was not high on the Israeli's priority list. Or he could call to the American for assistance, but if it turned out to be just another hole in the ground he'd have to live with the American's sarcasm. He'd have a look himself.

He stuck the gun into the grave and pushed the raincoat toward the rear.

A hand reached out of the depths and grasped him by the wrist, paralyzing him with fear. Before he had a chance to cry out, he was yanked head first into the pit.

Hecht stepped back and the Israeli's head slammed down to the bottom of the grave amid pieces of rotting wood, mud-caked bones and stones. Hecht winced at the sharp crack as the heavy-set man's neck snapped. Good, better than he'd planned, one down without a sound, one to go.

Hecht twisted the handgun out of the Israeli's grip, checked to determine that the barrel was free of mud, retrieved the car keys from the coat pocket, then using the body of the Israeli as a step stool, Hecht, wet, cold, and mud-stained, climbed out of the grave.

He stationed himself to the side of the opening in the chapel wall where he could see the road and the parked cars and still remain hidden. Sooner or later the other agent would investigate, but he would be wary and Hecht would have to be very careful.

Time passed. A car door slammed and Hecht risked a look. He was coming, gun in hand, sniffing the wind like a hunter.

Hecht stretched out flat on the ground alongside the wall just inside the opening. If he were lucky he'd get off the first shot before the other noticed him. His hands were mud-caked and cold and the unfamiliar gun felt slippery and clumsy. One shot, that's all he would get.

Hecht waited.

And waited.

Stupid, stupid, Hecht screamed at himself, of course the shooter wouldn't enter the ruin at this opening. Too obvious. There were other breaks in the chapel wall and he could easily enter through any one of them. Where was he? The hair on the back of Hecht's neck stood on end, expecting the fatal shot. He had to chance it. He rose, crouched low, then dashed out of the chapel.

The shooter was nowhere in sight.

Hecht backed against the outside wall of the chapel, listening to the blood roar through his own ears. Oh, that was close. He flattened himself against the wall, trying to watch both corners and the opening in the wall at the same time.

He waited. In the distance a crow circled and cried.

There it was—the soft squish of footsteps through the wet grass, just on the other side of the wall. Wait. Wait.

If the shooter chose to stick his head out of the side opening, Hecht had him. Even if he noticed the open grave and went to investigate, Hecht could slip in behind him. A couple of quick shots and it would all be over.

Crunching footsteps walking faster now. The shooter had seen the open pit.

Hecht stepped into the opening. The American was bending over the open grave. Hecht had a second, no more.

Hecht raised his weapon and fired, and fired again. The American tumbled soundlessly into the pit.

"And goodbye to you and all the other patrons of this establishment…"

Hecht dragged the gate on top of the grave and covered it with the raincoat. Then he anchored the plastic covering with a few large stones and camouflaged everything as best he could. Days, maybe weeks, would pass before the bodies were discovered.

He trudged back to the road and found the Mercedes with four flat tires. He laughed. Irish son-of-a-bitch, I believe you now. You're capable of anything, even finding a new species.

He retrieved his luggage from the Mercedes then climbed into the Austin Mini. He had no idea which way O'Donnell had gone, maybe north toward the border. He had a few bullets left in the plastic piece of crap they called a gun, more than enough to take care of business. Caked with grave mud, soaking wet, Hecht still managed to hum as he rammed the car into gear and spun away.

36

Lord Creighton of the Royal Ulster Constabulary the Northern Ireland police force, set the bottle down on his desk with a little flourish. "There you are, Charles, nothing but the best for you."

The chancellor of the University of Northern Ireland examined the label. "Remy Martin. I'm impressed, Willie. Very nice, indeed."

Creighton poured and both ceremoniously savored the first sip.

"Well, Charles, I know it's foolish to ask what brings you to Belfast so late in the afternoon," Creighton said, "because you'll tell me when you're good and ready."

"Yes, of course. This is first rate cognac, Willie. I had n o idea you chaps were so civilized."

Lord Creighton waited.

"It's about that O'Donnell matter we spoke of some time ago—"

"Yes?"

The chancellor paused to frame his sentence carefully. "I've had some second thoughts and I hope it's not too late to reconsider."

"What do you mean?"

"Call off your dogs, Willie. I should never have involved you in this affair at all. It's a university matter, and if O'Donnell's work offends Whitehall then the dispute is between Whitehall and the University. The Royal Ulster Constabulary has no stake in the controversy."

Lord Creighton leaned back in his chair and sipped his cognac. "Strange," he said, "but when you called I had a hunch you were going to bring up the O'Donnell affair."

"The point is, Willie, I'm supposed to be the chancellor of the damn University. The chancellor. I have an ethical, maybe even a moral, commitment—"

Lord Creighton laughed out loud. "Jesus, Charles, since when have you taken that post seriously? Am I talking to the same man who helped himself to a cool half million pounds on the Council Board? To the man who signed the Major-Jones contract?"

The chancellor nodded his head. "I know, I know, but this is different."

"In what way? A job is a job, and both of us know how we got the jobs."

The chancellor agreed. "Everything you say is true, Willie, but there's something about this job—"

"There's something about every job." The head of the R.U.C. breathed deeply and continued. "This one of mine has plumbed the depths of my inhumanity but I've still managed to keep a sense of morality, an ethical perspective—"

Now the chancellor laughed. "That's what you say, but how do others see you?" He sipped his cognac and had no intention of quarreling with his friend, but he had to win this one. "Once I read if one gazes too long into the abyss, the abyss gazes into one. The University has gazed into me and in some ways it has changed me."

Lord Creighton appraised the face of his friend with the eye of a policeman. "You're up to something, I can tell, what do you want me to do?"

"Remove yourself and your organization from the O'Donnell case, expunge all records of our interference. The University will deal with O'Donnell in our own way and to everyone's satisfaction."

Again Creighton laughed out loud. "Charles, we won't get anywhere till you stop trying to have me on. Now enough of this blether and tell me what you're really up to."

The chancellor's hurt expression quickly gave way to a grin. "All right, Willie, we'll do it your way. You know, both of us claim to be astute politicians, but damn the one of us is acting the part."

"Yes?"

"The Yanks have a saying that it's not over till the fat lady sings. Well, Willie, lad, the fat lady is walking out on the stage, clearing her throat." The chancellor sipped the cognac. "We're losing their war, Willie, the Republicans will reach an accommodation with Whitehall and Dublin and a new kind of Ireland will emerge."

"Aye, I see evidence of that every day," Lord Creighton said.

"Our position grows more untenable. How do you want to be perceived in this new Ireland? Personally, Willie, I want to keep my job, it pays well, but unless my faculty perceive me more as an academic than a politician, I may not have a job."

"Is there a message for me somewhere in your lecture, Charles?" Lord Creighton said. "I hope so or all your blether is lost on me."

"You asked me why I drove into Belfast. Here's my answer, to urge you to think about your own situation. Think of the future. Only even-handed justice will save your position, and let's hope both of us have enough time to change people's perceptions of our job performance."

"I've tried to be even-handed," Lord Creighton said, "and look what it's brought me, a vicious Unionist backlash, sectarian murders, and an enraged constituency." He glared at his friend, rose, and walked to the window. A fitting end to a bleak day. He stared through the rain-streaked panes in silence.

"You're closer to the situation than I am," the chancellor said, "so you must have guessed that the charade is almost over. You're too good a politician not to reach the same conclusion: the Brits will pull out; it's inevitable, Willie."

"How long do you think we have?"

"Long enough."

The R.U.C. chief turned and faced his guest. "The O'Donnell matter has been taken out of our jurisdiction," he said. "M15 and M16 want the man, and so do a number of other parties. He may not even be alive."

"Where is he now?"

"We lost him in the Republic. Our sources in the Irish police tell us he may have been—ah—killed by the Mossad."

"The Mossad? What the hell are they doing in Ireland?" the chancellor asked. "Let me bring you up to date. Your sources are wrong. O'Donnell was alive early this afternoon and on his way to Northern Ireland."

"Is that so? He's across the border, then?"

The chancellor looked at his watch. "He'll wait for dark. If your people don't get to him before the security forces, he's a goner."

"He's a goner anyway. M15 told me they wanted him alive or dead; dead would be more convenient."

"How long will it take you to alert your organization to take O'Donnell into custody?"

"Maybe an hour," Creighton said, "but you know as well as I do there's always some bugger who won't get the message. Let me understand you: you're asking the R.U.C. to intercept O'Donnell and take him into custody to protect him from British Intelligence?"

"I want you to make sure he arrived safely at the University."

"Why, for god's sake?"

"Because he's one of my faculty, he's done nothing wrong, and if M15 get their hands on him there will be world-wide repercussions from the academic community. M15 may get their man but we'll take the heat and pay for it dearly."

"All right," Creighton said, "I hope you know what you're doing. We'll do our best but don't get your hopes up. If I know British Intelligence, he won't get across the border alive if they don't want him to."

37

The mother cracked open the door and eyed Seamus. "Whatta yez want?"

"Is your son in, Mrs. MacAndrews?" Seamus asked.

"Who's askin'?"

As if she didn't know. Seamus showed his identity card. "Can I come in a sec?"

"We're havin' supper. Whatta yez want?"

Seamus' eyes danced over her shoulder, flicked about in the darkness beyond the door. "I'd like to have a word with your son."

"He's not in."

"I just saw him back there."

"Whatta yez want wi' him?"

"Police business. Now will you have him come out here to answer a few questions or would you rather I come back with a summons?" Seamus' eyes stopped dancing and riveted the mother's. She lowered her head.

"Now," he said.

"Scaffy!" the mother screamed over her shoulder. "There's a peeler out here awantin' you."

Both heard the window slam at the same time and the mother glanced at Seamus to see if he knew what it meant. He did.

Seamus bolted around the side of the house in time to see Scaffy MacAndrews racing across the field to the stream behind the distillery. Run, you over-grown scunder, run, I know where you're going and I'll have you in a minute.

Seamus took his time crossing the field. Muddy water squished over his shoe tops and he swore under his breath. His feet were already freezing with cold. Now he's have to walk around with wet feet till his shift was over.

A cluster of paint-peeled sheds stood across the stream on the opposite bank. Seamus looked around for a place to cross. Stepping stones off to the right. He danced across, light as a feather, and up the other bank. A ballet.

Which shed? A test, was it, to see if the peeler had enough powers of observation to pick the right shed on the first try?

Thank god most of the scuts he dealt with were short on brains. The trampled grass path to the door shouted, "We're in here!"

Seamus kicked in the door.

Four strapping youths stood in line waiting for him. Seamus picked out Scaffy MacAndrews and said, "I'd like a word with you. The rest of you can go."

"Not fuckin' likely, they can," Scaffy said. "You say what you have to say and then bugger off. We don't like peelers here, do we?"

The others grinned and moved closer to Seamus who didn't budge an inch.

"All right," Seamus said, "have it your way. Can you account for the whereabouts the night Constable Burke was murdered?"

"That's for you to fuckin' find out, Sherlock, isn't it?" Scaffy said to his grinning companions.

"You don't have to answer now," Seamus said, "I can take you in where the atmosphere will help clear the mind. One way or the other you'll answer; I don't care."

"Och, there's another way you haven't mentioned," Scaffy said. He was about a head taller than Seamus, so when he drew his arm back to swing he exposed his stomach at just about punch-height for Seamus.

Seamus, who had fought lightweight in his youth, didn't seem like much of a challenge but he remembered a few basics. His eyes were on Scaffy's stomach, the solar plexus, the seat of pain. He balled his fist, pistoned it forward about four inches, flexed his wrist and twisted on impact. The most damage for the least wear and tear on the hand. Actually, Scaffy was soft as a pillow. He dropped like a stone and crumpled in pain.

"I'm sorry about that," Seamus said, eyes flicking across the faces of Scaffy's gang, "but I've a right to protect myself, haven't I? A couple of you—you and you—get him on his feet till he answers my question."

Scaffy stood on rubber legs, bent over holding his stomach. Spittle ran down the side of his mouth.

"You didn't like Constable Burke much, did you, Scaffy?" Seamus asked.

Scaffy straightened up and drew his arm back again. One of his friends grabbed it and pinned it to his side. "Tell him, for christsake, before he gives you another kib. He's a flamin' boxer, can't you see?"

Scaffy tried to scowl but it turned into a grimace of pain. "No, I didn't like the bastard, but I didn't kill him."

"Where were you the night Constable Burke was murdered?" Seamus asked.

"Portrush," Scaffy mumbled.

"Can you prove it?"

"We were all there," one of the gang said.

"Can you prove it?"

"Shut up, youse!" Scaffy warned his gang.

"Can you prove it?" Seamus repeated.

"Fuck youse, Scaffy," one of the gang said, "they ain't worth goin' to jail for. Aye, we can prove it. We were with girls, five of them, all night."

The rest of the gang nodded their agreement.

"Is that right, Scaffy?" Seamus asked.

"Aye," Scaffy mumbled, "but don't tell their families."

"Don't worry. If your story checks out," Seamus said, "this is as far as it goes. I want names and addresses, all in confidence."

Ten minutes later Seamus left with the information scratched on an crumpled piece of paper he found on the floor. Next stop, the Burkes.

Mrs. Burke opened the door and invited him into the small parlor. She served him tea and inquired about his family. Seamus finally broached the subject.

"Maguire and I have been assigned to Phil's—your son's—case," he said. "We're going to find out who did it, so we are. Maguire's out questioning some of the Loyalist organizations; I volunteered to talk with you and himself."

"Well, I'm glad you did, Seamus. Phil always had a good work for you, so you must be a decent man." She paused. "Himself hasn't been the same since Phil passed away. He's up in the bed now. Do you want me to get him?"

"If he can get up—"

"Oh, aye, it'll be good for him to talk about it. He's got it all choked up inside him."

Old Mr. Burke creaked down the stairs and sat opposite Seamus. "Bearing up under all the work?" the old man asked, grasping with both hands the mug of hot tea his wife gave him.

"Oh, aye," Seamus replied, "it's a job, isn't it, when so many are walking the streets I'm grateful for the work."

"Aye, God have mercy on us all, I don't know what the end of it will be. Are you making any progress with Phil's shooting?"

"That's why I'm here. Did you know Maguire and myself were assigned full time to the case?"

"I heard that. An awful thing, so it was."

Seamus took a few wrinkled sheets of paper from his inside jacket pocket. "I know you've been over this before," he said, "but witnesses seem to remember a bit more each time they tell their story. Will you tell us again how it happened?"

"Aye," the old man said, and the pain of recall set his chin trembling. He recounted the events of a night forever etched in his mind.

"Did you see anything of a face at all, anything of a shape, or a walk, anything that might give us a clue, anything at all?" Seamus asked.

"Nothing, son."

"A license plate, maybe?"

"Och, it was pitch dark, so it was, and the car had no lights. I chased it half way down the street, but I didn't have time to get on me and I was in my bare feet—"

Seamus thumbed furiously through his sheets. "You say you chased the car half way down the street—"

"I was in my bare feet, so I was," the old man said, "so I couldn't run that fast, what with the—"

Seamus looked at him. "Are you sure, Mr. Burke? I have your previous testimony taken on the night of the shooting and it doesn't say a word about chasing after the car."

"But he did, so he did," Mrs. Burke said, reaching over and grasping the old man's trembling hand, "I saw him, I did, indeed, and him in his drawers, and running something awful for a man of his age. He must've forgot to mention it, he was that upset."

"Did you tell this to anyone else?"

"Tell what, son?"

"That you ran after the car?"

"No, there's been nobody here. You're the only one that's asked me."

Seamus slowly folded his papers and slipped them into his inside pocket. "Well, I won't trouble you any longer, but I may be back."

"You're always welcome, Seamus," Mrs. Burke said.

Before driving away Seamus sat in his car and ran the old man's testimony through his mind again. Something was wrong here, something terribly wrong.

38

Kevin reasoned if Hecht knew about the borrowed car then he could have learned of the arrangement to leave the car at Duffy's in Bundoran. So Bundoran was out. Kevin changed direction and drove northeast.

Three hours later he reached Killinell and stopped at one of two pubs on the main street. He ordered a Guinness, sensing a sudden tightness in the atmosphere when he tried to strike up a conversation with the patron standing next to him. His Belfast dialect was a dead giveaway.

"Bearing up under the weather?" Kevin said.

The stranger looked him over before answering. "Where are you from? We've had a fairly decent day here."

"Drove up form Kinsale. Trying to get to Coleraine."

"You can cross the border here."

Kevin sipped his Guinness and then took the bull by the horns. "Aye, I know, but I can't go through the check point. My passport's a fraud."

The stranger gazed ahead and tossed off his Guinness as though he hadn't heard a word.

"If they pick me up it's an English prison for me," Kevin said, glancing around to see if anyone else was listening to the conversation.

The stranger set his glass down then walked away without saying a word, but Kevin noticed that two men left the bar and took up positions on either side of the door. Kevin would not be allowed to leave until something else happened, but what? He ordered another drink and waited.

About fifteen minutes later a gray-haired man in his fifties, stocky, red-faced, planted himself at the bar, shouldering Kevin out of the way. Kevin nodded and smiled and made room for the stranger.

The stranger ordered a drink, then without looking directly at Kevin asked, "Who are you?"

"Kevin O'Donnell from Coleraine."

"Are you I.R.A.?"

"No."

"Why are you on the run?"

How could he answer the question in a sentence or two? Kevin chose his words carefully; his life hung on the words.

"Ah, I'm from the university of Coleraine. I've done some research that the British government considers, ah, dangerous, I suppose. The Israelis are trying to get rid of me and the Brits want to cart me off to a English prison."

The stranger remained silent.

Kevin continued, "I know it sounds strange, but—"

"Do you take us for bloody fools?" the stranger asked. He had lost two men last year, two good men, when they offered to help a stranger from the North; an outlaw Protestant group ambushed them for their trouble just this side of the border. It wouldn't happen again. "If you don't do better than that, it's a loanen for you with a bullet in the head."

Kevin's mind raced.

"Will you make a couple of phone calls?" Kevin asked. "There's a Dr. Burke at the University who'll vouch for me, and my brother, Barry O'Donnell, in Belfast."

"Write me down Barry O'Donnell's phone number."

Kevin scratched it on a piece of paper and the stranger disappeared into a back room to make the call. Kevin sipped his drink but it didn't lie well in his stomach. Catching Barry at home would be a miracle, especially early in the evening when he usually made the rounds of his constituents, a drink here, an argument there, arranging for payment of rent or a bag of coal. Outwardly calm, Kevin's stomach churned and even the Guinness couldn't soothe it.

The stranger returned and once again shouldered Kevin out of the way. He leaned close to Kevin and said in a low voice, "Barry said to watch yourself. M15 is looking for you. He also said to turn yourself in to the first R.U.C. you see—"

"R.U.C.? Is he daft?" Kevin said. "They'll turn me over to the Brits before you can say Jack Robinson. Barry must be—"

"Listen, you hard-headed wee shit—Barry's words, not mine—the chancellor of your university has made a deal with the R.U.C. to bring you in. The only way you'll stay alive is to get to your university in an R.U.C. armored car, and I might add, you're flamin' lucky you're related to Barry O'Donnell or you'd be having a ride in a different kind of car."

"When do we start?"

The stranger motioned and the two men guarding the door came over to the bar. "Get him a bicycle," he said, "and take him to Daly's bridge. Watch yourselves; I don't want a repeat of last year."

"Will you see that my car is returned to its owner?" Kevin asked.

"Write it down and we'll do the best we can. Good luck to you."

An hour later, under a moonless sky, Kevin shook hands with his guides, slipped the strap of his bodhran over his shoulder, and pushed his bicycle across a field capped with evening damp. He reached a narrow stream and paused. Across, lay Northern Ireland. Well, it would be hours before he dared risk another halt so he turned his body toward the hedgerow and urinated.

As soon as the urine moistened the ground, a alarm clanged and lights blazed on at a security outpost just two miles away.

39

No forgiveness, he was on his own, he couldn't return home, and if he didn't soon disappear, he was a dead man. But he was confident of his skills, maybe a bit overconfident. If people realized just how stupid the so-called intelligence agencies of the world were— and that included the Israeli's—they'd die laughing, or crying. Paid informers who were turned two or three times, or just lied; agents and handlers with mediocre minds and sophomoric imaginations (John LeCarre to the contrary); leaders and ministers making important decisions they were incapable of comprehending...

Hecht sat in a bathtub filled with about four inches of lukewarm water, scrubbing with soap that barely lathered, splashing water around his body, under his arms, trying to dig the graveyard mud from underneath his fingernails.

Well, they wouldn't get him.

He climbed out of the tub feeling a bit cleaner but reluctant to put on the same dirt-stained clothes. Tomorrow he would get a complete change. For now they would do.

He had asked the owners of the bed-and-board, a pleasant old couple in their sixties, for something to eat but all they offered him was cold pork and Irish soda bread, both of which turned his stomach. He settled for a pot of hot tea and something they called scones and jam. He would have eaten the bark of a tree (if he could've found a tree) he was that hungry. He sipped the tea and nibbled at the scones and spread a map of Ireland on the dresser top.

No doubt the Mossad would expect him to cut and run; anyone in his situation would. To Spain. To Italy. Eventually to South America. Not Hecht, m aster of the unexpected, of the in-your-face arrogance, the shooter of shooters. The survivor.

Like some New Yorkers who spend their traveling lives underground in subways, Hecht had trouble comprehending direction on a map. North, south, east or west—who knew which way the subway was going? Who cared? He studied the map, trying to work out and remember route numbers.

The ferry out of Larne to Stranraer suggested all sorts of possibilities. The Israelis would expect him to fly out of the country, south, no doubt; instead, he would take a leisurely cruise into the lion's den. Larne would be lightly guarded, if at all, but first, he would finish his assignment. Professional pride, stubbornness, just plain anger at the Irishman, call if what you will, he would first head north to Coleraine and settle his debt.

Having decided on a course of action, Hecht felt much better. He lay down, clothed, on the bed and napped for a few hours. In the dead of night, in good spirits, he squeezed into the Austin Mini and started north toward Coleraine. This time next week, who knows, he might be managing a bookstore in Glasgow and looking forward to a normal life.

40

"Contact!"

The sergeant shook the sleeping lieutenant till he opened his eyes. "What? What?" the lieutenant rolled sideways out of the bunk, fully dressed except for boots.

"Contact, boss."

"The lieutenant ran his fingers through his jet black hair. "Where?

"Sector 5, one of the piss-ah, urine detector number 3, boss. The platoon's ready."

Fully awake now. "Right, sergeant, thank you."

The rumble of diesel engines vibrated the ground beneath their feet. "Load up, boss?"

"Yes." The lieutenant pulled on his boots then unfolded his sector map and laid it on the bunk. "Sector five. "Let's see, dismount here, three sections, radio silence except on contact or emergency."

"Right, boss. We'll ride with—"

"Corporal Crane." Lieutenant Amen of 2 Brigade, Glosters strapped on his pistol belt. "And tell that bunch of wankers if I catch a tom even thinking of sleep I'll have his balls for high tea."

The iron gates of the fortress-like R.U.C. station swung open and two armored personnel carriers, down shifting, belching blue smoke, thundered across the barriers into the night Surprisingly agile for their size and bulk, the vehicles skimmed along a side road, lights dimmed, kicking up huge clumps of wet dirt.

"All the men accounted for?" the lieutenant asked above the roar of the engines.

"Yes, boss, all present except Sneads. I told you about him."

"That malingering bastard."

"Right, boss, we ought to get rid of him. Crane is always a man short."

"No, that's what he wants. We'd all like to get out of this hell hole. Let's not send the wrong message to the rest of the platoon. Sneads will do his turn, on his feet or on his arse he'll finish his tour of duty with the rest of us."

"Right, boss."

Ten minutes later the vehicles jerked to a sudden stop, the troops quickly dismounted and formed themselves into three sections; each section led by a corporal fanned out across a dark, hilly meadow. The lieutenant and his sergeant watched in silence, then followed the rear guard. The sergeant whispered into his radio.

"3 Lima here. Acknowledge."

"30 LimaA here, out."

"31 LimaB here, out."

"33 LimaC, out."

The sergeant clicked on his radio. "Roger, stay alert, it's a bright night and we're on open ground for the next mile or so. We're easy pickings, 3 Lima out."

The damp cold chilled Amen to the bone. He clenched his jaw to keep his teeth from chattering and walked faster to increase circulation. A dog barked in the distance, a cloud-veiled moon flooded the field with half-light, silhouetting the shadowy forms of men moving against a silver-grey sky. Amen had led enough of these night patrols along the border to know that death and disfigurement came screaming out of the dark without warning. Stay alert. Silent night, Irish night—

"Contact!"

Toms freeze. Sergeant on the radio.

"Okay. Who was that? Say again."

"33 LimaC. Contact."

"What do you have, Crane?"

"About a hundred yards to the front. Male pushing a bicycle across the field."

"Bullseye!" Amen said. He took the transmitter from the sergeant. "Crane, Lieutenant Amen here."

"Yes, boss?"

"That's our man, I'm sure of it. He's probably not armed but don't take any chances. Outflank him and be sure to cover all avenues of escape. We're to your left rear and coming up fast. Get him, Crane, and treat him like any other Paddy until you know for certain. Take no chances. Understood?"

"Yes, boss."

"Go get him. We'll be there in ten minutes."

When Amen arrived, Kevin was spread eagle on the ground with a tom's foot on his back. Amen said, "Are you Kevin O'Donnell?"

"Aye, I am."

"Get your foot off and let him up," Amen said to the tom. "Have you searched him?"

"Here's his stuff."

Amen shone a torch on Kevin's wallet and papers. "Not short of money, are you?" He rifled through the rumpled bills. He paged through the soiled pages of Kevin's research project. "What's this?" he asked.

"The source of all my trouble," Kevin said, "a bit of research that no one wants to see in print."

A tom thumped Kevin in the back with his rifle butt. "You bloody well mind your manners and answer the lieutenant properly."

"That's enough," Amen said. "What's that?" he asked nudging the bodhran with his foot.

"A bodhran, an Irish drum," Kevin answered, "and my only source of entertainment."

"Well," Amen said, "you won't need it where you're going. M15 will provide all the entertainment you can stand." He kicked the bodhran out of the way.

Kevin reached down and picked up the bodhran. A tom immediately slapped it out of his hands and it rolled to Amen's feet. Amen raised his boot. Two or three stomps and the issue would be settled. He paused in midstep then booted the bodhran back to Kevin. "What the hell," he said, "pick up your damn drum. Okay, let's go home."

"Secure his hands?" the sergeant asked.

Hesitation. "Not necessary," Amen said. "The only thing dangerous about him, according to M15, is his ideas and we can't secure those."

The troop carriers lumbered back to the R.U.C. station and Kevin was pushed into a guarded room with a cot, chamber pot, and bars on the windows.

"I'd like my personal belongings back," he said to Amen.

"Would you?" Amen replied, slamming and locking the door.

The next morning Kevin was still asleep when breakfast of plain bread and hot tea was pushed through the door. "Come on, professor, sort yourself out," a tom said, "we've made you a brew."

Kevin was sipping tea and nibbling at the bread when Amen entered. He tossed Kevin's bodhran off the cot and sat down.

"I read your stuff," he said. "Very interesting. Is that what M15 is losing their knickers over?"

Kevin nodded. "Absurd, isn't it?"

"Yes, but I can see why the politicians are a little nervous, the bunch of arse-licking Neanderthals."

"What happens to me?"

"Unfortunately, it's out of my hands. M15 is coming for you later this morning." He glanced at the chamber pot. "We can do better than that." He opened the door and summoned the tom on guard outside. "Find someone to take this man out and let him have a decent wash-up."

Amen touched Kevin's arm. "Be careful of M15, professor, they may be Neanderthals but so are their methods."

41

They're actually playing "good copper", "bent copper" with me. Unbelievable, one of the most sophisticated intelligence organizations in the world and even a child can see through their charade.

The two M15 agents had arrived about one hour ago. The "bent copper" had the first try.

"You stupid bastard, did you actually think you could cross the border undetected?" He stood over Kevin with his crotch so close to Kevin's face that Kevin could see a small stain on the fly of his dark blue trousers.

"We know you didn't cross without help and we know the people who helped you," he continued, "so pick them out of this pile of photos. If you don't cooperate, I'll personally kick the living shit out of you and relish every minute of it."

He tossed a number of Polaroid snapshots on the bunk and spread them out. Kevin recognized the red-faced man who had arranged the crossing and one of the others who had brought him to Daly's bridge.

"I never saw these people in my life," Kevin said. "Maybe if I had, I wouldn't be here."

The agent back-handed him across the face, a bruising, heavy-handed wallop that brought tears to Kevin's eyes. "You cheeky bastard."

"That's enough," the "good copper" said, "I'll take over, go somewhere and cool down."

The "bent copper" glared at Kevin and said, "I'll be back."

The "good copper" rearranged the photos on Kevin's bunk. "Sorry, he has a short fuse, that one. Take another look and don't insult our intelligence. We know all of these people are I.R.A., we just want to know who helped you cross the border. Why do we want to know? Because if they're over there we can stop looking for them over here. Does that make sense? Now I'd advise you to pick out somebody, anybody, it doesn't matter."

"I never saw these people in my life."

"Okay." The agent gathered up his photos. Tone of voice indifferent. "Is there anything you need?"

"I was promised a shower and a change of clothing," Kevin said, "I've been wearing these for days."

The agent hesitated. "I don't know about that. I'll have to find out."

He left the room and Kevin had a chance to run his fingers over his bruised cheek. It felt puffy and hurt like blazes.

The "good copper" cracked open the door and said, "Okay, I found someone to do your laundry, the guard outside will take you to the shower. Pound on the door when you're ready to pass out your soiled clothes."

Kevin shed his mud-stained clothing, underwear and all, and rolled them inside his trousers. He knocked on the door and called, "Okay, ready."

The guard opened the door slightly and said, "Pass them out. Is this the lot?"

"Everything. I'll need a pair of trousers or something to go to the shower."

"Right. I'll be back in a sec."

"Hurry, it's freezing in here."

"Right."

Kevin waited. And waited.

The "bent copper" crashed into the room. He looked at Kevin and said, "what the hell are you doing standing around naked?"

"I—ah—" trying to cover himself with his hands "—I gave my clothes to the officer outside to be laundered."

"Laundered? Are you serious? There's no laundry here. Well, anyway, Lady Godiva, we're going to be fingerprinted, so on your horse and let's go."

"Without my clothes?"

"Did you surrender your clothes willingly?"

"Aye, I did, but—"

"Then move your fuckin' arse before I drag you out by the hair. You have to be fingerprinted, that's normal procedure; if you want to walk around naked, that's your business."

Kevin reached for the blanket on his cot but the "bent copper" yanked it out of his hands and pushed him out of the door into a narrow hallway. R.U.C. constables, male and female, and British security forces brushed past each other. Kevin tried to cover himself with his hands.

"That's not much to show off, is it?"

"Actually, I've seen more meat on a sparrow."

"Look at his arse—like two wee eggs tied in a hanky."

Mortified, Kevin glanced downward, prodded from behind by the "bent copper" who paraded him through the busiest sections of the station.

"Make way, stand aside for Professor Kevin O'Donnell in full university regalia," the copper joked, nodding, grimacing, steering Kevin around corners and through doorways with a hand on his shoulder.

Cold. Breath steaming. Laughter and taunts. Finally into a small room where a female constable said, "I can't fingerprint you if you won't take your hands off it."

More laughter.

"Put your hands up here on the shelf," she said, stepping on Kevin's cold toes with her heavy work shoes. "Oh, sorry."

She fingerprinted Kevin, smudging his arm and chest with ink. "Sorry," she said and dropped the ink-smeared paper towel on his genitals. "Oh-oh, sorry, again."

This won't do, Kevin thought. I'm behaving exactly the way they want me to, embarrassed, nervous, apprehensive. Well, okay. I can take care of that.

He dropped his hands to his sides and pulled himself up to his slender five foot nine inches, and bowed. "Thank you, madam," he said and turned to the agent, "When you're ready to continue, sir. Shall I go first?

"By all means," the "bent copper" said, stepping aside and waving Kevin past him.

Back through the hallways, more laughter and pointing, freezing cold, only this time Kevin walked erect with his hands at his sides, head up, smiling, nodding, freezing—

"Just a goddamn minute, you." Lieutenant Amen, in his combat fatigues, automatic rifle slung over his shoulder, confronted the "bent copper" as he and Kevin almost collided at the door to the Ops. Room.

"What the hell's the matter with you, parading a naked prisoner through the corridors?"

"Naked was his own idea, I just took him to fingerprinting, that was my idea," the agent said.

Amen looked at Kevin for an explanation.

"Och, they tricked me out of my clothes," Kevin said. "I was stupid enough to trust them." Teeth beginning to chatter, breath steaming.

Amen said, "Give the man back his clothing."

The "bent copper" shrugged. "They were filthy, we burned them. If you want him to have clothes, you'll have to supply them yourself."

"You know damn well we only have regulation uniforms." Amen held his temper in check. "See that he has something to wear while he's here at TAC Headquarters or our OC will have a word with your OC."

Voice rising. "I suggest you mind your own fuckin' business, lieutenant, or M15 will have a word with you."

"What, and relieve me of my duties here in this garden spot of the world? Oh, the thought of it brings tears to my eyes." Then Amen shouted, a fearsome sound in the narrow corridor. "Get this man clothes, you simpleton." People disappeared into doorways.

Amen slowly, deliberately, stepped aside and allowed them to proceed.

The "bent copper" said nothing until they reached Kevin's room. "Open the door," he snapped at the constable standing outside. He pushed Kevin inside. "There's plenty of time to get information out of you," he said to Kevin, "you bet I'll make the most of it. And don't get your hopes up; there won't be any clothes coming in here, at least not till you decide to cooperate. At this temperature it shouldn't take long."

Kevin wrapped himself in a blanket and sat on the edge of his bunk. The damp cold soon penetrated the covering and he decided that walking might help, not that there was much room to walk. He paced up and down and around the room until his feet were numb with cold. He might as well get used to it because they weren't getting any information from him. After a while he sat down and rubbed his freezing feet. Walking wasn't the answer; maybe push-ups.

The door opened and the "good copper" entered, feigning surprise that Kevin had not received clothing of any sort. "That's damn strange," he said, "I'll have a look into that, meanwhile I've a few photos I'd like you to see."

He covered the bunk with enlarged photos of the bodies of women and children burned, blasted and mutilated beyond recognition. Kevin turned away.

"No, look at them," the "good copper" said, "the filth that would do a thing like this is not worth protecting. This is what happens when the I.R.A. plant their bombs among civilians. You can put a stop to this."

Kevin looked again and a surge of anger swept over him, anger at the barbarians who could do this to innocents, and then disgust that his government would use the atrocities of the recent Balkan war to serve their own ends. They hadn't even bothered to disguise the Slavic signs in the bombed-out store windows.

"I wouldn't protect people who inflict that sort of cruelty," Kevin said, "never."

"It's one thing to look at pictures," the agent said, "and another to see it close-up."

He opened the door and said to the constable outside, "Let's have it."

A small bundle was passed into the room, the agent laid it on the cot and unwrapped it. Kevin barely contained his anger and disgust.   A child's arm, severed just above the elbow, frozen, fingers blue and curled, frost-glistening shreds of flesh clinging to the raw edge, lay in the center of a towel stained with frozen blood.

Get hold of yourself. This pitiful wee thing is from a hospital operating room. Look at the next surgical amputation.   This rotten bastard thinks nothing of using the dead limbs of children to get what he wants. Get hold of yourself, play his game. Oh, Jesus, I'm ashamed to say I belong to the human race.

The "good copper" solemnly re-wrapped his exhibit and passed it out to the constable. He gathered up his photos and sat down on the edge of the cot and waited.

Kevin sat beside him, wrapped in a blanket, cold, clenching and unclenching his fists, fighting off the urge to jump on the bastard and strangle him.

"I'd hoped you'd cooperate," the "good copper" said, "and make it easy on yourself. There's enough bloodshed to last us for a while without spilling your own unnecessarily."

"What do you mean?"

Silence. "The only reason I was sent along with his nibs was to protect you. He's ruthless, human life means nothing to him, he's a throw-back. If you don't give him something he'll break your bones, fingers first, I've seen him to it. His sister was killed by I.R.A. bombers, you've no idea how he hates them."

"What more can I say?" Kevin asked. "I've told you I don't know these people, I'm not even from this part of the country."

The agent rose. "I hear you're an intelligent man, a professor. You ought to know a psychopath when you see one. Give him somebody, anybody. You're on your own in this place, no one can protect you, and he'll be back in an hour or two. Plenty of time to think about it."

The agent left, closed the door, and then opened it again. "By the way," he said, "If it's money you need and a new position at a university in England, that can be arranged. Think about that, too."

Kevin bundled the blanket around him and paced the floor. Bitter cold. He picked up the bodhran and examined the bullet hole in the goatskin head, not too had, he could have it recovered; the rim was nicked where it had struck Hecht in the face. Now there was a piece of work. If Hecht showed up in Coleraine he'd have him arrested for attempted murder. Coleraine? He could be in an English prison tomorrow.

The door creaked open and the R.U.C. guard slipped into the room. He tossed a bundle of clothes on the bed, including shoes, an R.U.C. cap, and Kevin's well-thumbed papers.

"Get these on you quickly and listen while you're doing it," he said. "There's an eagle patrol—"

"What's that?" Kevin asked struggling into trousers two sizes too large.

"Helicopter patrol. It's leaving in fifteen minutes and I'm on duty at the gate. You're to slip through after the Security Forces and walk—mind you, walk—to the side barricade. The constable there is expecting you. Proceed down the street to McCann's Chemist, go inside, and change out of this uniform. There'll be a car waiting to take you north."

"Why are you doing this?"

"God knows," the man replied, "we've orders from Belfast to get you back to Coleraine. Here are your papers and your money." He pointed to the bodhran. "You can't take that, looks too bloody obvious, don't you think? Just leave it in the room here." He paused. "One more thing. MI5 is being kept busy by our people for a short time. If something should go wrong and they catch you, keep your mouth shut or you'll never leave here alive. Do you understand?"

The Wessex thundered, rotors swooshing, olive drab fuselage rattling and vibrating on the pad.

"Ready, boss."

"Right," Amen said, "load up."

Two rows of toms filed into the chopper, bent over, as the enormous blades sliced through the air inches above their heads. The sergeant climbed in and Amen looked around before following. Out of the corner of his eye he saw an R.U.C. constable walking toward the barbed wire-canopied barricade. Something not quite right about that man.

Amen climbed into the chopper and it wobbled off its pad, turned, and sped away, climbing, into the overcast sky. Five minutes later descending over the DZ it came to Amen what had caught his eye and he almost burst out laughing. A bodhran hung by a strap from the R.U.C. constable's shoulder.

"Jesus, I wish I could just walk out of here, too," he said to his sergeant.

42

The ruddy-complexioned man sitting across the huge desk from Maria seemed ill at east, which, in turn, added to her own discomfort. Strange, too, for the chancellor usually appeared in command of the situation. She folded her hands on her lap and waited for him to tell her why he had summoned her to his office.

The chancellor fidgeted with a paperweight, a pewter griffin, which he passed from hand to hand, turning it over and running a finger along its irregular surfaces. "Ah…Professor Burke…ah, I hope I didn't take you away from important duties."

"No, Your Grace, my mind's on little else these days other than the safety of Dr. O'Donnell."

"Yes, of course, that's one of the reasons I asked you to come here. The latest intelligence I have places that gentleman somewhere between here and the border, closer to here. I've been assured by the R.U.C. that everything has been done to facilitate his return." He paused. "In spite of problems with U.K. Internal Affairs, I might add. So you see risks have been taken and positions jeopardized, this has been no easy task I assure you."

"I'm deeply grateful," Maria said, "and so is the University."

"Yes…ahem…and that brings me to the second reason for our meeting, to…ahem…seek your counsel regarding the steps one might take to assume a more…ahem…active role in the academic affairs of the University."

"There are others much more qualified than I to offer advice."

"Maybe so but I doubt it, and certainly no one that I would trust not to take advantage of the situation, if you follow my meaning."

Maria leaned a little closer. As a psychologist alert to the many little nuances of human behavior, Maria thought she detected a quality usually missing in her infrequent encounters with the chancellor—sincerity. What was this strange and aloof man trying to say?

"How may I help you?" she asked. No qualifiers. No judgment. Counselor to client. Private. Comfortable. "How may I help you?"

The barriers seemed to crumble, the huge desk shrunk, the chancellor relaxed and leaned toward her, "How does one go about becoming a better university chancellor, one, perhaps, who is trusted and respected by the faculty?"

If Maria was surprised, her face showed none of it. A client had asked her a question of deep importance to him and she had to respond, help him find an answer his own question.

"I'm not sure how to reply," Maria said, "so I'll ask you a question. What gives you the sense that you're in control of this institution, how do you know, in fact, that you are the chancellor?"

Pause. "I suppose it's because I make decisions that affect the entire university."

Silence.

Then, "Of course," the chancellor said, "perhaps that's the answer. All right, suppose I would be willing to share with the faculty certain of the responsibilities entrusted to me as chancellor. How does one begin to do that?"

"By sharing the power, Your Grace."

Silence. "But how would one know if such power would be used wisely?"

"Trust."

The chancellor played with the griffin, turning it over, passing it from hand to hand. "Where do I begin?"

"At the bottom, I would think," Maria said. "Our division will meet soon to elect a new head, Professor McKensie's term has expired."

"I shall attend," the chancellor said, "and henceforth I shall become more visible to my faculty." Pause. "However, there could be a problem with your division, a question of Dr. O'Donnell's future with the division and the university. I know I've made certain commitments to you and Dr. O'Donnell regarding his reinstatement and promotion which I could certainly impose on the division by fiat. Or do I hear you say that these decisions should be shared with the faculty?"

Aha, you sly old rascal, you place me in a situation of confidentiality and then you maneuver me into recommending that the faculty take responsibility for actions that might threaten your own security. Neat. You've hoisted me with the petard of my own self righteousness. How did you do that?

"Yes, Professor Burke?"

"Those are exactly the kinds of decisions in which the faculty should participate," Maria replied.

"Then you'll hold me blameless should your division faculty decide that Dr. O'Donnell deserves censure for neglect of duty, or even suspension, dismissal?"

"I'll hold you blameless."

"Even though I'm duty-bound to recommend the decision of the faculty to the Board?"

"If that's the faculty's decision then I'll certainly hold you blameless, as will Dr. O'Donnell, I'm sure. He would not want to work in an atmosphere of suspicion and resentment, nor would I. If you can clarify that situation, both of us would be grateful regardless of outcome."

Maria walked back to her office in the crisp noonday cold, bare-headed to the wind, sifting the events of the meeting through blue-eyed logic. His Grace, the Duke of Pelham, consummate politician, had certainly rid himself of a potentially vexing problem but he had opened the flood gates of democracy and the university would never be the same. The careers of Kevin and herself, however, would rest in the hands of their peers. How would the faculty react to their new-found power?

The departmental secretary indicated a small, slender man sitting on a chair next to the radiator. He rose as the secretary announced his presence.

"This gentleman has been waiting to see you, Dr. Burke."

They shook hands. "I'm Maria Burke. Would you care to come back to my office?"

"Thank you."

"I'm Oliver Teague," he said, "from Purdue University in the States, perhaps you've heard of Purdue?"

"Oh, yes, in Indiana," Maria said, "and what brings you to Northern Ireland?"

"The work of Dr. Kevin O'Donnell."

"Oh? He had hoped that was a well-kept secret."

"I know he's out of town but I've heard that you're his friend. Could you direct me to his dig? I'll be most careful, I'll disturb nothing except take a few photographs. I ask this because his project appears to be similar in many ways to one of my own."

"Oh? In that case perhaps you should wait for Kevin."

"When do you expect him?"

"In a day or two."

"I'd be happy to wait but I've taken for only a few days. If I promise to do absolutely nothing except look around, would that satisfy you?"

"I suppose so," Maria said, "I couldn't keep you out anyway, the cave is open and the wee string of yellow tape across the front doesn't discourage too many people."

"Good, it's a deal then. I'll not touch a thing unless I talk with Dr. O'Donnell. Now if you would be good enough to point me in the right direction—"

"The whereabouts of Kevin's cave is hardly a well-kept secret around here," Maria said, smiling, and rough-sketched a map on a page of university stationery.

"Thank you, thank you so much."

Maria watched him go and reached for the telephone.

Hecht had what he wanted and hurried to his car.

43

An impenetrable fog crept across Lough Neigh, smothering the reeds along the shore, blanketing twilight with a drizzly shawl. Low on petrol, exhausted, Kevin sighed with relief when a small sign announcing bed and breakfast materialized out of the fog. He almost missed it as it hovered ghost-like over a grey stone wall leading to a driveway and the shimmering glow of window lights. Enough running for one day. A nice supper and then sleep. Sleep.

"Good day to you, or should I say good evening?" Kevin said to the woman in the doorway, a little boy peeping out from behind her skirt. "Are you open for business?"

"Och, no," she said, "the fishing season's long passed."

"It's a terrible night to turn away a stranger in need," Kevin said, smiling, "would you make an exception? If you don't you'll have me on your conscience all night."

The woman ran the experienced eye of an innkeeper over Kevin. "Well, there isn't another place for miles. All right, up the stairs, first door to your right. Will you be having supper?"

"Aye," he said, "if it's not too much to ask."

"You're from Belfast, then?" she asked.

Perhaps elocution lessons could help him lose the lilting drone of the Belfast streets. "Aye, I was."

"Where in Belfast?"

The inevitable question to pinpoint section, thus religion. "Off the Donegal Road, near the M1 roadway."

"Oh, and what do you do now?"

"I'm a university teacher."

"Queens?"

"No, Coleraine."

"The new one."

"Not so new."

"Supper'll be ready at half-past five."

"Thank you."

Kevin threw himself on the large, bouncy bed, tempted to close his eyes and let the day slip away but the hunger pangs would not be denied, so he washed his hands and face in the hall bathroom and did what he could to smooth the wrinkles from the clothes provided him by the R.U.C.. Half an hour later, on the dot, he descended the stairs to a warm dining room where a place had been set for him at the evening meal.

"I'm Nora Breen," the landlady said, "and this is my son, Alex, who'll be four years old next week."

"I'm Kevin O'Donnell and I'm happy to meet you, Nora and Alex. Now, I'll thank you to pass the potatoes, Alex."

"I hope you like roasted chicken. We've had our share of fish for the year, haven't we, Alex?" Nora said. "Chicken for a change. What brings you to Loch Neagh, you don't look like much of a fisherman, Mr. O'Donnell."

"Och, I don't fish at all," Kevin said, "and please call me Kevin. I've just returned from America and I'm driving back to Coleraine."

"Do you hear that, Alex, he's been to America." She looked carefully at Kevin, noting his ill-fitting clothes. "You have no luggage?"

"No, and it's a long, sad story; you don't want to hear it. The chicken is delicious, Mrs. Breen."

"Call me Nora."

Alex spoke only once, to ask for a glass of milk. He sat next to Nora and she watched him carefully, too carefully, as she made sure he ate his small portions of food.

"Well, you're a beautiful big lad for your age," Kevin said, "you must like to fish, living on Lough Neigh."

Alex paused in mid-chewing, his eyes watered, and tears coursed down his cheeks. He never made a sound.

Nora glanced sharply at Kevin and said with her eyes, change the subject. She brushed the tears from Alex's cheeks and said, "Och, now, we promised, didn't we?"

"Aye, mum," he whispered.

"Would you like to go and watch the telly?"

"Aye."

Alex ran off and Nora settled back to her own dinner. She ate in silence and Kevin gave her plenty of space. When she had cleared away the supper dishes, she asked, "Would you like a cup of tea?"

"No, I think maybe you and Alex would like a minute to yourselves."

"Och, no, have a cup of tea with me, it's not often I've a chance to talk with another adult, with the winter coming on and all."

"If you're sure—"

"I'm sure."

She served tea and sat staring into the glowing coal fire till she realized Kevin was watching her. "Oh, excuse me, Kevin—all right to call you Kevin, isn't it? -you must think we're strange, Alex and me, the way we carry on, but you'll just have to put up with us."

"Och, they tell me I'm a strange one myself."

"Andy, my husband, was drowned last year, last July 14, when he tried to rescue two drunk Derry men. They hired a boat and motor and swamped in a storm. Andy went after them but they managed to swamp him, too. All three drowned a hundred yards off shore and I knew nothing about it till Andy's body washed up a few hours later. He couldn't swim." She paused, "Boats for hire, a strange business for a man who couldn't swim, don't you think?"

"I'm sorry, Nora, I'm so sorry."

"Alex and I've kept the business going, and we're doing all right, the two of us. But the season's short, you know, and the winter's long."

"You're a brave woman, Nora," Kevin said, "and a beautiful one, someday another Andy—"

"There'll never be another Andy. He was just about your height and build, I don't know where you got those clothes you're wearing but our Andy's will fit you much better, so before you go to bed I want you to pick out something…"

The bed was warm and soft and Kevin was sound asleep before the clock in the hallway downstairs chimed 8 o'clock. Oblivion. He remembered hearing the door creak open and the hallway clock strike two, he even remembered hearing his name whispered—

269

"Kevin…Kevin."—but he didn't blink fully awake till someone touched his hand. He sat up.

"I've made a wee pot of tea and the fire's beautiful and warm downstairs," Nora said, she wore a white terrycloth robe and her dark hair flowed past her shoulders, her eyes were blue-awake and waiting for an answer.

Kevin must have looked at her strangely for she said, "Tea's all," and he understood, for she left the room on tiny slippered-feet and he followed without a sound.

He sat on the carpet before the fire, in Andy's robe, and listened to her talk for an hour—about the business, about the problems with the bait people and how she decided to net her own, about little Alex and how much he missed fishing with his daddy, about the cost of coal, about next season and the boats she hoped to add to the fleet. Then it was his turn.

He talked about his work but mostly he talked about Maria and how sorry he was about Phil's murder.

"And you let her go back by herself," Nora said, "just when she needed a hand to hold across the long Atlantic?"

"I should have listened to my heart," Kevin said.

"What heart?" Nora scolded. "Sure, you don't know your heart from your hormones. Your heart's with Maria Burke, even I know that just from listening to you. You find that girl and tell her…"

Little Alex walked out, mostly asleep, dragging a blanket. They tucked him between them and then lay down themselves.

"Good night, Kevin O'Donnell, you're a good man but a bit thick."

"More thick than good," Kevin mumbled and dropped off to sleep. Only once did he stir during the night when little Alex became uncovered and he reached over and tucked him in.

Dawn.

"Get up, Kevin, get up and get on you, hurry, they've found you."

Instantly awake.

"There's four soldiers in a Land Rover and they're searching your car." Grey light streaking the curtains. "There's a boat with an electric trolling motor anchored at the dock. Go along the shore to your left till you see a rocky outcropping, about a mile. Go ashore and you'll see my white van, it says "Breen's Landing" on it. Here's your stuff and the key to the van, now off with you, they're coming. Don't forget to anchor the boat, and you can return the van when you're ready. I won't need it off-season."

"What about you?" Kevin said, struggling into Andy's clothes. They fit perfectly.

"Don't worry about me. I'll tell them you went jogging and I'll make them breakfast while they're waiting for you to return."

Knocking on the front door.

"Off with you now," she said, "out the back door. Here, don't forget your papers and your bodhran."

"Why are you doing this?"

She kissed him on the cheek. "Because you look so handsome in my Andy's clothes."

271

44

If he had stayed at Maghery at the foot of Lough Neigh and then drove toward Coleraine, he would surely keep west of the lake and drive straight north, right? Wrong. That's what they'd expect, so Kevin doubled back toward the east, skirting the eastern shore. Toward late morning with a bit of sunlight perched cold and high above Aldergrove Airport, Kevin stopped for petrol and to use the restroom at a roadside station.

On the way back to the van he caught a slight movement off in the grass to his right and noticed the gun emplacement manned by a single British soldier. Were there was one there were more. Kevin said, "Hi, there."

"Lo, moite," the tom mumbled, trying to smile, "how's about you?"

"Can I get you something, a mug of tea?"

"Not allowed."

"Well, try to keep warm."

"Roit, moite."

The old van rattled and bounced along the road, agile for its age, no doubt Andy kept it in tiptop condition. It smelled of fish and petrol and the heater worked so well that even on low Kevin shut if off occasionally. He planned a westward jaunt past Clogh Mills, and then straight north to Ballycastle, through Ballycastle to A2, the coast road, and he was practically home, thanks to Nora Breen and her old van.

He saw the roadblock about a quarter mile this side of Ballycastle limits. It wasn't an army or R.U.C. checkpoint because private cars blocked the road. Kevin recognized it instantly: a Protestant paramilitary gang flexing its muscle.

He swung the van quickly through an open farm gate, but not quickly enough, cars screeched from the side of the road and raced toward the gate. Kevin didn't know where the rutted farm road led, nowhere, he suspected, so the only alternative was to turn right across the field parallel to the roadblock and hope for an intersecting road ahead.

The old van bounced and jolted and took to the open terrain better than the pursuing cars, one of which had already skidded out of control on the rain-soaked earth.

Kicking up streams of mud, occasionally skidding and fishtailing, bucking like a bronco, motor racing, the white van passed the roadblock on the other side of the hedgerow, and raced for what Kevin hoped would be a road going off at right angles, marking the edge of the field.

He guessed right. The van crashed through a few strands of barbed wire and dropped about two feet onto a road. The back wheels churned momentarily without catching as the drive train cut through the earth, but the van freed itself and, skidding and twisting, scattering mud behind it, roared easily up a hill as if grateful for the traction. The pursuing cars, both of them, teetered off the embankment, wheels spinning, unable to go forward or back.

Kevin glanced in his rear view mirror. So much for that, and it'll take them a while to pull themselves together. But his elation didn't last long. Glancing again in his mirror from the crest of the hill he saw two cars screeching around the corner about a mile behind. Nothing to do except race for Ballycastle.

Into town, around the circle, squeezing past parked cars, dodging pedestrians, Kevin had his hands full avoiding the congestion. The cars behind were closing quickly. If they forced his van onto the sidewalk or into cars parked on both sides of the narrow street, people would be hurt. Already a traffic warden waved his arms in desperation.

Then, behind him, out of a side street rolled a hay wagon, a large, ungainly tractor pulling a trailer piled high with hay. Oblivious to everything except steering his load through a tight turn and avoiding traffic coming from both directions, the driver, totally unconcerned, brought all traffic to a standstill. The traffic warden raced out to untangle the confusion of cars, delivery vans, bicycles, and pedestrians.

Just a car or two ahead of the traffic jam, Kevin turned left, raced uphill to the first intersection, turned left again, and back tracked through the outskirts of the town to the coast road that angled off about two miles ahead. If the congestion in town held for about five more minutes maybe he could lose his pursuers.

The coast road twisted and turned high atop the Antrim cliffs along the arm of the Atlantic called the North Channel. Breath-taking vistas, heart-stopping plunges to the ocean below, twists and turns that demanded full attention. Both hands on the wheel, ignoring the view he had often admired, Kevin glanced into the rear view mirror and caught a glimpse of his pursuers, far back but gaining.

Faster. He had to risk it all, he wouldn't stand a chance with thugs who specialized in sectarian murder and killed without qualm, selecting the softest, easiest targets they could find, brutes disowned and dishonored even by their own people.

Kevin steered the van down the steep slope into Ballintoy, practically standing on the brake as the road turned sharply onto the main street. A line of small buildings spaced less than a mile along the road, no place to go, no place to hide. It would have to be Ballintoy.

He skidded the van into the parking lot of the Harp Bar at the near edge of town and drove behind a large van delivering drinks to the establishment. Then, hidden from the road, he eased his van behind a shed full of fishing tackle and the remnants of scaled and gutted fish. Two fat cats, one black, one orange, refused to budge from their lounging places in the center of the path, forcing Kevin to park with the rear end of the van protruding slightly from behind the shed.

The driver of the drinks van, a well-built, red-haired man in his middle fifties, watched as Kevin maneuvered the van behind the shed just minutes before three cars screeched around the turn and then raced on the narrow stretch of road through town.

Kevin had no choice. He approached the driver of the van and said, "You're wondering what's going on, aren't you?"

"No," he replied, "I'm wondering what you're doing with my friend Nora Breen's van."

"You know Nora, do you?" Kevin said. "Och, it's a small world, isn't it?"

"Not when you deliver wines and spirits all over Northern Ireland, including Breen's Landing. Now don't take me for a fuckin' eejit and tell me what you're doing with Nora's van."

Small talk wouldn't satisfy this man so Kevin told him about staying at Nora's and all that followed. Then Kevin said, "Would you be going toward Coleraine? I'd be grateful for a lift. And maybe I could leave Nora's van here till I get a chance to drive it back to Maghery."

The driver hesitated, then, "You wait here a minute and stay out of sight of the road."

He went inside the Harp Bar and didn't return for about ten minutes. When he came out he smiled and carried two bottles of beer one of which he handed to Kevin. "Nora says to leave the van and give me the keys," he said. "She also said to mind your bloody bodhran and take it with you, and if you're going to help me deliver crates and cartons, you'd better put something on over Andy's clothes. She expects them back in the same condition she gave them to you. There's a work jacket in back of the van. Put it on."

His name was Boxie Lennon and he didn't mind telling Kevin that he was an Orangeman from the Pride of Drummond Lodge in Newry. "And if you're going to ride with me, wee Fenian-me-lad, you're going to work for it. Now, mind you, if them that's chasing you stops us, you keep your yap shut and let me do the talking."

They delivered to off-licenses and public houses scattered along the coast road. Boxie sat at the counter supping his pint of "fuel for the road" while Kevin struggled with heavy crates of spirits. When they concluded deliveries, Boxie usually came out with a bottle of beer for "wee Finian-our-boy" and a happy grin, and then they were off to the next stop.

About mid-afternoon Boxie asked, "Do you fancy a fish supper?" When Kevin replied he could "eat the arse out of a rag doll" he was that hungry, Boxie pulled the van into the parking space of the Union Supper.

He ordered two fish suppers, a Black Bush for himself and a pint for Kevin, "our boy". "That'll hold you, won't it?" he said. They had hardly finished eating and were enjoying the sup when the door burst open and a group of youths piled into the small shop and milled around the counter, boisterous, shouting out their orders. One of them approached Boxie.

"Is that your delivery van outside?" he asked, leaning over the table so that the handle of the gun stuck into his belt was visible.

"Aye, i'tis."

"Have you seen a white van anywhere along the coast?"

"Can't say as I have," Boxie replied, fixing the youth with a stare as cold as the North Channel.

The young man looked at Kevin, nodded, and went back to his friends.

A short time later Boxie and Kevin left. Late afternoon, a few more deliveries, a few more drinks, they sang as the miles rolled under the van:

"With a toot on the flute and a twiddle on the fiddle-o-,

Up and down the middle like a herring on the griddle-o…"

The van, empty and bouncing, rocked into the gathering dusk.

Kevin said, "You can drop me off here, Boxie."

"Here? Sure there's nothing here but bloody ocean."

"Aye, it'll have to do." Kevin gathered up his bodhran, reached over and shook hands with Boxie. "Go n'eirigh an bothar libh," he said.

"Now what the hell does that mean, in your bloody Fenian tongue?"

"May the road rise to meet you. Thank you, my friend."

"Goodbye, wee Fenian-our-boy, and good luck to you."

Singing down the path to the water's edge, hurrying along the sandy track at the foot of the cliffs to the cave entrance. Teetering inside. Quiet, echoing darkness. Groping for the ledge and the lantern…aye, flickering match, the yellowish glow flowing into the darkness. The old desk, the sleeping bag, the candle stubs, the rows and rows of skulls, patient, waiting…

"Good evening, ladies and gentlemen, and wee babes. I'm home."

45

Kevin woke with a headache, and no wonder, with all the "fuel" he had consumed. He lay quietly for a few minutes trying to get his bearings in the darkness of the cave. He had lost track of time and he was too comfortable to take his arm out of the sleeping bag to look at his watch. He rolled over to go back to sleep.

A match flickered in the darkness and a kerosene lantern sputtered and then glowed steadily.

"No, don't get up," Hecht said, "I want you zippered up and helpless." He laughed.

Hecht sat on a camp stool just out of lantern range, yet near enough for Kevin to see his shadowy outline.

"Can I sit up, then?" Kevin asked.

"Yea, but I want to see both hands. No funny stuff, Irish. Do you know how long I've waited for this moment, to catch you with your pants down", he laughed, "with no way out, right by the balls."

"You owe me," Kevin said, "I could've killed you back there."

"I owe you nothing, you Irish pain in the ass." Hecht got up and walked over to the rows of skulls, keeping a watchful eye on Kevin sitting up in his sleeping bag. "But I have a deal for you, anyway. Whether I kill you or not won't make a damn bit of difference to the Israelis. No matter what they promise, they'll try to kill me, and don't bother to ask why. I know them. I came in here to kill you, but if I do, what do I get? Nothing; personal satisfaction. Now, what do I get for *not* killing you? A way out, maybe."

Kevin watched his movements. A trick, another one of his slick deceptions.

"Irish, I may be a lot of things, but first I'm a pragmatist."

Pragmatist? "What do you want?" Kevin asked.

"If I shoot you in here I'll start a manhunt that could be troublesome," Hecht said, "but make no mistake, if I wanted to, I would, and if I have to, I will. But when I look around here at what you do and what you get for going it—", he paused, "—as one misfit to another, I admire your work, and I wish I had your luck."

"Okay, now what do you want?"

"I want—", pause, "—I want to walk out of here. I want your word that you won't identify me from pictures, sketches, ever. I want you to forget you ever saw me. You get to keep on living and I get a chance to leave the country. You forget my face, I'll forget yours."

"You tried to kill me," Kevin said, "and god knows who else you've killed. I'm supposed to forget all that?"

"Hey, you're in no position to be picky. I'm offering you your life for mine, and I've got the gun. That's a fair bargain. If you turn it down, I'll shoot you now and take my chances."

Period. Kevin recognized the staccato of finality. He had pushed his luck to the brink.

"It's a deal." Kevin said, looking up at Hecht, fascinated by the little red dot that danced about on Hecht's forehead. The red dot. Hecht couldn't see it or feel it.

The roar of the shot blasted away thousands of years of pristine silence and a gaping hole burst open on Hecht's forehead. He tumbled back and collapsed into the rows of skulls.

Kevin unzipped his sleeping bag and sprang to Hecht whose body was flopping spasmodically on the dirt floor amid scores of skulls. Hecht momentarily grasped Kevin's hand, held on, then slowly relaxed as his body calmed and lay still. Kevin felt for a pulse. There was none.

"Damn you, Maguire," Maria shouted, "that wasn't necessary. He wasn't even armed."

"What's that in his hand, a banana?" Maguire said. "Move away from him, O'Donnell."

Kevin rose and looked at Maria and Maguire. "Didn't you hear him say he wasn't going to shoot?"

"We heard," Maguire said.

Maria wrung her hands, upset by the violence. "He came to my office and asked about you," she said to Kevin. "I recognized him from your description, so I called the police. I was only trying to protect you, Kevin, I didn't know Maguire was going to shoot him."

Kevin looked at Hecht, small and still, sprawled among the skulls in the flickering glow of the kerosene lantern. "Maguire, is it? Well, Maguire, that killing was unnecessary but I suppose it makes little difference to you."

"Oh, let's stop the bloody nonsense." Maguire walked over to Hecht and twisted the gun from his hand. "I was going to kill him anyway no matter what he said or did."

"Why?" Kevin asked.

281

"Because I need his gun," Maguire examined it. "Bloody plastic." Then he said, "You see, Hecht killed the both of you with this gun and I had no choice; I had to kill him."

"What are you talking about?"

Maguire pushed Maria over to Kevin, leveling Hecht's gun at both of them. "Now I'm going to finish what I started with Phil Burke."

"What are you saying, what about Phil?" Maria said.

"I'm saying he was a traitor to his country and his service, he was soft on papists, a collaborator—"

"You know who killed Phil?" Maria asked.

Pause. Lantern light flickering off Maguire's pale face. "If you think the North is going to be ruled from Dublin, if you think we're going to put up with one of our own who gives aid and comfort to the enemy— aye, I killed Phil Burke and I'm going to kill the two of you, and then I'm going to make sure our deceased friend here gets full credit for it."

Seamus' voice spoke softly out of the dark of the passageway. "I don't think so, Maguire. I've got one of those night-shooting thing-a-ma-jigs, too, and the wee red dot is plastered all over the back of your thick skull."

Maguire knew Seamus; he gave up without a word. Seamus disarmed and cuffed him.

"You followed us here," Maria said to Seamus, "how did you know—"

"Och, I've been on to him since he told me in Florida about your da chasing after the car that shot Phil," Seamus said. "That information was not in your da's deposition and when I asked your da about it, he said he'd told it to no one." Seamus pocketed the guns. "The only one who could've known about your da chasing the car was him that was in the car."

"What are we going to do about him?" Kevin asked, indicating Hecht.

"I don't know," Seamus answered, "M15 and M16 have sent us all sorts of bulletins about him so I'll let them that's getting paid for it figure it out."

Seamus left, pushing Maguire ahead of him. Kevin looked at Maria for a second then reached out and took her to him. He held her and covered her face with kisses.

"Are you that glad to see me?" she asked.

"Oh, I am indeed." Kissing her, running his hands through her hair, brushing away the tears. "I wouldn't tell a soul but you," he said, "but I cried for Phil, too."

She sobbed quietly and he didn't try to stop her. "I thought you might," she said.

Minutes passed.

"Are you laughing?" he asked. "Aye, you are. What's so bloody funny?"

"You are," she whispered, "do you know you're naked?"

He looked down. "Holy Mother of God, have I been standing around her like this?"

"Aye, you have."

They left a short time later. Maria said, "Drop me off and take my car and disappear for a few days. There's too much going on at the University that involves you right now. It's better if you're not there."

Kevin hesitated.

"Does it bother you, love, about not going to the University?" she asked.

"Och, no, I wasn't thinking about that." He paused. "I was thinking, it just doesn't seem right to leave him lying in there."

"I heard the both of you talking. I think you did your best, now let it be."

"Aye, I suppose so."

"Do you love me?" she asked.

"I love you."

"What about—what's her name?"

Kevin looked out across the water. "Och, don't be too hard on 'what's her name', she taught me a lot."

"Older women usually do."

After driving Maria home, Kevin traveled back along the coast road to Ballintoy Harbour and turned at the winding road leading down to the quay. A good a place to disappear for a few days.

46

"Maria?"

"Kevin! Where in blazes have you been?"

Kevin held the phone away from his ear. Softly, "You're shouting, love."

"Och, I'm sorry, I'm just so agitated that you didn't phone."

"You told me to get lost for a few days."

"That was a week ago," Maria said. Quietly. "Where are you now, what have you been doing?"

"I've been staying at Ballintoy Harbor and I've had the grandest time."

"Can you meet me at your cave in about an hour?" Maria asked.

"Oh, aye, I'll be there."

Maria held her shoes in her hand and strode purposefully along the path at the foot of the cliff, skirting boulders of black basalt half-buried in the sand. High above the rolling swells, the gulls played tag with the wind, now and then a gannet dove straight down from the sky and buried itself with a tiny splash in the sea. The smell of salt spray and sea weed filled her nostrils, her heart beat faster, and—

There he sat, sitting on a rock with the sea swirling at his feet, looking for all the world a part of the landscape. She could tell by the way he rose and came to her that he was upset.

"They've cemented me out," he said, stretching his arms to encompass the range of cliffs.

"Yes, darling, come here and I'll show you," Maria said.

The entrance to the cave no longer existed, in fact, the concrete so cunningly blended with the rock that only someone familiar with the place could tell that an entrance had ever existed. When the concrete dried thoroughly and weathered, the entrance would disappear completely.

"When did this happen?" Kevin asked.

"The day after. I didn't know about it myself till the chancellor told me. All part of the deal, he said."

"And my papers and stuff?"

"They're inside."

"My bodhran?"

"Inside, too." She pulled him by the hand. "Look."

A brass plate was fixed in the concrete high up on the face of the cliff out of reach of the tide. Barely discernable from ground level were the figures, "1014NT".

Kevin looked on in silence. Then, "What happened to—"

"M16 took charge of everything. They said his name was supposed to be Joseph Hecht, but that wasn't really his name. The Israelis said they never heard of him and knew nothing about him. No one claimed him."

"So, where is he?"

"He's inside, too. M16 said since this was a tomb, one more body wouldn't make any difference. I think the Israelis had something to do with it. They had to make him disappear totally, completely, and M16 obliged them."

"And he's sealed up inside with my stuff?"

"Just as well," Maria said.

Kevin stared at the blank concrete wall. "Do you mind if I stay here for a while and—"

"You can't, Kevin, you have too many responsibilities now."

"What do you mean?"

"You're the new chairperson of the division; the faculty elected you unanimously."

"Och, away!"

"And the chancellor took it to the board and they confirmed. So you can't sit out here thumping your drum anymore and letting things go to sod."

Kevin looked out to sea. "I don't know if I really want that, I'm not a very responsible person, you know."

She reached out her arms and hugged him. "Oh, god, what does it take to make you join the real world? She hugged him tightly, kissing him, then—"Do you see that brass plate up there? It says, '1014NT', but that's just a National Trust catalog number."

Kevin held her face between his hands and kissed her on the tip of the nose. "So what?"

"Next to that number in the ledger of the official archives is the notation that the cave is to be re-opened in the year 2100 and the real name permanently affixed. The name by which it will then be known forever, my darling, is 'O'Donnell's Boneyard'. Your paper and notes will go to a museum, your gift to your great grandchildren. People from all over the world will come to see Dunluce Castle and the Giant's Causeway and O'Donnell's Boneyard. Is that the respect you wanted? Will that do?"

"I think a hundred years from now I won't give a damn, but I like the idea of grandchildren. I'm ready to start work on that."

They walked hand-in-hand back to the road, skipping around little fingers of the sea that trickled across the sand. Only once did he look at her, wondering, but apparently she didn't hear it, the beat of the bodhran, fading away, dancing out to sea with the gulls and gannets—

     Thus-thud-da-da-thud-
        Da-da-thud-
        Da-da-thud-
           Thud-thud—da—da—thud—
                Da—da—thud—
                    Da—D—

About the Author

Seamus Thompson was born in Belfast, Northern Ireland, and received his early education there. He received his B.A. from Wagner College (New York), his M.A. from Teachers College, Columbia University (New York), and his Ed. D. from the University of Florida. He taught in the Florida public school system and served on the faculties of the University of Florida (Gainesville), Indiana State University (Terre Haute), and retired from the University of South Alabama as Professor Emeritus.

Upon retirement, he settled in New Port Richey, Florida. He continued to write both nonfiction and fiction until his death in 1997. He wrote three nonfiction books, *Instructional Communication* (Van Nostrand Reinhold, 1969), *Beyond Words: Nonverbal Communication in the Classroom* (Citation-Scholastic, 1973), and *Practical Basic for Teachers* (Charles E. Merrill, 1985).

O'Donnell's Boneyard, is one of several fiction books that were written and never published during his lifetime.